How to split up & stay in one piece

Surviving divorce and relationship breakdown

Rosie Staal

Editor Roni Jay

WHITE
LADDER
PRESS

Published by White Ladder Press Ltd

Great Ambrook, Near Ipplepen, Devon TQ12 5UL

01803 813343

www.whiteladderpress.com

First published in Great Britain in 2008

10 9 8 7 6 5 4 3 2 1

13-digit ISBN 978 1 905410 29 3

British Library Cataloguing in Publication Data

A CIP record for this book can be obtained from the British Library.

Designed and typeset by Julie Martin Ltd
Cover photos by Jonathon Bosley
Cover design by Julie Martin Ltd
Printed and bound by TJ International Ltd, Padstow, Cornwall
Cover printed by St Austell Printing Company
Printed on totally chlorine-free paper
The paper used for the text pages of this book is FSC certified.
FSC (The Forest Stewardship Council) is an international
network to promote responsible management of the world's forests.

FSC
Mixed Sources
Product group from well-managed
forests and other controlled sources

Cert no. SGS-COC-2482
www.fsc.org
© 1996 Forest Stewardship Council

White Ladder books are distributed in the UK by Virgin Books

White Ladder Press
Great Ambrook, Near Ipplepen, Devon TQ12 5UL
01803 813343
www.whiteladderpress.com

Contents

Acknowledgements

My greatest debt of gratitude is to the many people who so selflessly relived their own experiences when answering the case study questionnaires upon which this book is based. Many of them asked for anonymity so I can only thank them here as a group, with due humility.

I am grateful to the professionals to whom I turned for advice, and in particular to Karina Leapman, Jane Moses, Kirsten Gronning, Trisha Stone, Jackie Walker, David Plimmer and Ariana Gee, who generously shared their knowledge and gave me so much of their time.

Finally, my heartfelt thanks go to David, my second and last husband, who put me back together many years ago and then ensured I stayed in one piece.

Introduction

Divorce is something that happens to other people. At the last count it was about 300,000 other people a year. We have become almost immune in this country to the impact of the shocking statistics of failure: one in three first marriages, one in five second marriages, but they don't involve us – they're just numbers. We hardly give a moment's thought to all those sad couples and their broken dreams. Nearly a third of a million of them, every year.

Until, suddenly, one day it's us. Whoever would have thought it could come to this? We have become a statistic ourselves.

So what's the best way to get back on track after this shattering, life-changing trauma? This book will help, lighting a path for you through the dark days and giving you direction and hope as you start a new phase of your life. Helping you choose the route will be many others who have been there before and who want to pass on the wisdom gained from their experiences.

Like you, their lives may have been broken, but they are all still in one piece – and so will you be.

CHAPTER I

Facing up to life without your other half

He may have mucked up my marriage but I wasn't going to let him muck up the rest of my life. I have things to offer – I need to be a functioning parent for my children – screwing myself up with resentment was not going to help. *Vicky*

She left me with £23,000 of debt on credit cards and cash drawn from the bank. I have at times become very depressed and have sat and had a good cry. In fact I still do, many times, trying to get my head round all the debt and the way I'm having to live my life. *Malcolm*

Recovering from adversity, which, in a nutshell, is what this book is mostly about, is all to do with inner strength. You've either got it or you've got to find it, and once you start to use it you begin to get better.

Finding it and using it are what you are most likely to need help with, and one of the best ways of doing that is to discover how other people have found and used that all-important inner strength as they've recovered from their own relationship breakdown.

Whether you are the one who has been dumped from the relationship or you've done the dumping, there is a lot to recover from. You may have been together for six months or 60 years, either way you and your partner have made memories together, you've moulded into each other's ways and thoughts, adopted each other's daft expressions and funny habits, but now it's just you, without your other half.

The first thing to absorb and keep reminding yourself is that this is not an ending. It's a beginning. You are now at the start of a new phase of your life. OK, it may not be a phase you'd have chosen, had you been given the choice, but the fact is you are where you are and you have got to make the best of it.

Sinking or swimming is largely up to you, but it must be assumed that you want to be one of the swimmers otherwise you wouldn't be reading this book. However, swimming with a confident smile on your face and a song in your heart is probably a long way off at the moment, so it's probably best to start with a few lengths of doggy paddle while you find which direction you want your efforts to take you.

It is true that you may be a statistic now – one of the 300,000 or so whose broken marriages zap them back from whence they came, into singledom, each year – but where your once-happy union may not have survived, you certainly will. How you survive, what your situation will be in, say, five years' time, what twists and turns your life will take now you are back in sole charge of your destiny – all these are imponderables. But by gaining knowledge, strength and insight along your journey you stand the best possible chance of feeling good about yourself and, in turn, feeling good about your life.

The expert says...

If you're the one who doesn't move out of the marital home, the compulsion to totally redecorate the house is complete. I know many people who, like me, have been up until the early hours of the morning and unable to rest until they have repainted the whole of the house. You have to do a certain amount of remodelling and making it your own, even if it's just your bedroom. That's critical.

Ruth, of Divorce Recovery Workshops

How you're likely to cope could well depend on whether you're male or female. According to a survey carried out in 2005 for the Yorkshire Building Society, divorce left 23% of men (and 20% of women) feeling devastated, while 46% of women (and 37% of men) were left feeling liberated.

More than two years after a divorce, 41% of men were still sad about the failure of their marriage, but for women the figure was only 33%. Possible reasons for this imbalance are women's greater willingness to seek help and to utilise coping strategies and the stronger ties they have with friends and family. Men are apparently more prone to seek solace in drink, work and the search for a new partner.

The survey questioned 3,515 divorced adults about the impact of their marital break-up. It found that nearly three-quarters of those who had separated more than two years ago were happier now, while splitting up within the last two years had left 57% of divorcees happier. The most significant trend highlighted by the research, however, was that women are overwhelmingly shown to handle divorce better than their male partners.

The part that others play

One of the best ways of recovering from something as personal and as potentially damaging as a broken marriage is to talk about it with someone else, preferably someone who has been through the same sort of experience. Learning how their relationship foundered and how they got back on their feet can boost your confidence. Knowing they've been able to put the traumatic times behind them and move forward to a new life shows you what's possible and what you could aim for.

This book is filled with the personal experiences of many 'break-up survivors', each telling the story of a different journey. Woven around them are contributions from people whose work involves rebuilding lives – counsellors, therapists, specialist lawyers, specialists in divorce recovery, and others – who give their views on how best to resolve certain issues.

The expert says...

One person, one partner or the other, is always in control. Couples who have become co-dependent who suddenly find themselves without the 'other half' can find coping with everyday life incredibly difficult.

David Plimmer, relationship counsellor

Our survivors have not held back in giving the sometimes quite harrowing detail of their stories. Starting with the causes of their relationship breakdown, we encounter:

- Rape
- Alcoholism
- Infidelity
- Changing sexual orientation

- Physical and emotional abuse
- Violence
- Child-snatching
- Drug abuse
- Out-of-control spending
- Mental illness
- Sexual problems
- Bullying
- Falling hopelessly in love with someone else
- Incompatibility, in all its many manifestations

Then we learn how the effects of the break-up radiated through their lives and how, in time, they came through to be the people they are today. The lessons they learned along the way are set out at the end of each case study, making it easy for you to pick and choose those bits of advice you think are most appropriate to you and your situation.

At the end of the book there's a summary of their advice in a Top 20 list of survival tips for ensuring you move seamlessly through the stages of recovery until you can confidently say "I'm a survivor, too."

In the meantime, it is important to remember ...

You are not alone

No, you definitely are not alone. However much you may think you are the only person in the world to be going through so much turmoil and heartache, rest assured you are not. Countless men and women have been there before and there are thousands in your situation right now. That doesn't make it any better for you, but when you wake in the night and are gripped with anger, fear, fury, loathing or sheer out-and-out despair, you can at least cling on to the thought that there are plenty of others tossing and turning in their lonely beds.

The expert says...

We're not taught about relationships, far from it. We're supposed to cope just with a mixture of luck and chemistry.

Trisha Stone, singles coach

Being in bed alone is one of the zillion things to adjust to: no more comfort from spooning your partner and no more waking up and saying "You'll never guess what I dreamt!" Equally, there's no more dismissing of those evil thoughts of carrying out a cruel-to-be-kind smothering act with the pillow. Yes, things may have got that bad but now you're apart and the dust, while not exactly settling, is probably not choking you any more.

Finding a way out of that dust cloud is what this book will help you do, but first let's cast a final glance over our shoulders at what you've been through. While you may not wish to be reminded of the recent past, there will be others reading this book at a different stage of their break-up who have a little catching up to do.

It's over and there's no going back

The parting is inevitable and now all you want to do is be rid of each other. However, it is likely that, depending on what has caused the break-up, you and/or your partner will be going through the classic phases of:

- Denial – "No, not me"
- Anger – "Why me?"
- Bargaining – "If you'll stay, I'll change"
- Depression – "So it really has happened"

- Acceptance – "This is what happened"

Once you reach the stage of acceptance – and it can take months or years – you can move on and create a life for yourself. Meanwhile, it is a tough call that when you are at your lowest, your strength and powers of endurance need to be at their greatest. This is because you are dealing with the fallout and it can be terribly distressing, especially when children are involved.

What you are searching for, through all the unhappiness, is a sense of justice. The next chapter should help you achieve that.

The expert says...

A quick checklist to help you start pulling through:
1 Become responsible for your own thoughts, actions and desires.
2 Stop blaming and shaming.
3 Find something to focus on which is positive and work towards it.
4 Let go – the worst will never happen.

Jackie Walker, divorce coach and NLP practitioner

RESIDENCE AND CONTACT – TERMINOLOGY

Common parlance in respect of residential arrangements for the children of separating couples includes the words 'custody' and 'access' – as in "I've got custody of the kids but he's got access every other weekend."

However, as a result of the Children Act 1989 courts make a Residence Order which says where the children will live (that is, not to whom the children belong), so the correct word is 'residence', not custody.

Similarly, a Contact Order requires the person with whom the child lives to allow the child to visit or stay with the person named in the order, or for them to have contact with each other. So, correctly, it isn't 'access' but a Contact Order which defines the time, place, frequency and other details of the arrangements.

In some instances, for ease of understanding, the words 'custody' and access' will occasionally be found in this book instead of 'residence' and 'contact'.

CHAPTER 2

A good way to get divorced

The impact of family breakdown is huge so we lawyers tiptoe along the line, hoping we are not leaning to one side more than the other. *Karina Leapman, family law specialist.*

It is not always the heartache or even the fact you are divorcing someone you (presumably) once loved that does so much harm to your family, but the way you get divorced.

Bitter squabbles over goods and chattels, finances and, of course, children, create long-lasting schisms, making future communication painful if not impossible and cutting off members of the wider family from each other. The process of divorce is a fertile breeding ground for family feuds, so that rants of blame and recrimination quickly become a familiar soundtrack not just in the unhappy couple's home but among their close relatives too.

One of the things that adds to the bitterness is the adversarial nature of the traditional divorce procedure: your solicitor versus their solicitor locked in an often futile exchange – two adults slugging it out to try and get the best result for their client. This tense and often expensive situation can go on for months until sometimes it is felt that only the courts can decide who 'wins' and who comes off second best.

If you don't fancy this combative kind of showdown you may find yourself having to back-pedal on some of your demands. Trying to be reasonable and agree to a compromise is always going to be a more stress-free way of going on, but be wary of conceding too much just because you want it all over and done with quickly. There is a middle course, and that's where legal advice can be invaluable.

Get yourself a good solicitor

When divorce is on the cards, the usual recourse is to put yourself and your future into the hands of a solicitor. "Get yourself a good one," everyone will tell you – but how can you tell good from bad?

"It isn't at all easy," says Karina Leapman, a family lawyer based in West Hampstead, London. "Someone who may be a great lawyer for one person could turn out to be a disappointment for another, because obviously every case and every person is different."

The expert says...

Karina's top five qualities to look for in a good lawyer, and thus a more bearable divorce procedure, are:

1 Being willing and able to communicate with their clients
2 Being a competent and knowledgeable family law specialist
3 Ensuring their clients understand the process
4 Understanding how important it is to 'gel' and empathise with their clients
5 Ensuring there's a failsafe system of either speaking to the clients when they call the office or making sure someone else takes a message and/or calls them back

"As lawyers we work in a traditionally adversarial court-led system," Karina says. "We are not taught how to deal with the emotional side, so we have to teach ourselves to develop other skills and also how to discipline ourselves not to go off at a tangent. It is very easy to become engrossed in a client's emotional problems, but actually by doing so you can become very one-sided and too subjective to be able to act for them properly. Also, a degree of objectivity is needed so that if necessary you can give clients advice that they don't want to hear.

"In family law there is a tendency for clients to change lawyers because they are being told things they don't want to hear," Karina says. "That's one of the most difficult tasks that a family lawyer has. Some litigators have an easier time of it but the impact of family breakdown is huge so we tiptoe along the line, hoping we are not leaning to one side more than the other."

Those who have been through a divorce before, and those who have been alongside others who have, will always swear that having a good lawyer is one of the fundamentals for a bearable divorce. "It's absolutely crucial if you want to come out of a divorce with your pride intact and anything to show for your years of marriage," says Katharine, 35, who pays tribute to her lawyer for securing her a handsome settlement when her marriage ended.

Paul, 51, says that if it hadn't been for his "first-class lawyer, who cost a lot at the time but saved me a lot more in the long run," he'd have been holed up in a measly maisonette facing the loss of half his pension in ten years' time.

The best way to find a good solicitor is to ask around and take up the recommendations of friends. Don't be blinkered by age or gender prejudice but go for one who has the right specialist knowledge and with whom you feel you could get on well. It will almost certainly save you time and money in the long run if you consult an expert in family or divorce law.

Vicky, 64, deliberately chose to see a middle-aged woman solicitor when she was getting divorced 15 years ago. "I hoped she might identify with my situation," she says. "In fact I chose my doctor for the same reason, but both of them went off work indefinitely with breakdowns – just when I needed them. The realisation and sad truth that I, with all my woes, was the common factor did not escape me."

However, it is possible to get a divorce without having to go through the sometimes lengthy and costly business of engaging a lawyer to take an adversarial stand. You could instead opt for one of the ways that promise rather more sweetness and light.

Three routes to no-court divorce

I MEDIATION involves face-to-face sessions with a neutral, often non-legal mediator who ensures you and your partner are given a fair and equal say. The mediator is not able or allowed to give you or your partner legal advice but is simply there as a facilitator.

Don't confuse mediation with reconciliation. Mediation [*for contact, see box at end of chapter*] is an option only once you and your partner recognise that your relationship has definitely broken down. It is not the forum for reconciling your differences.

Mediation sessions, which each last between an hour and two hours, are intended to help both sides work out a route to the future which is mutually acceptable and mutually agreed. They help find solutions to disputes in all types of relationships – married, co-habiting or civil partnerships – and may also include input from other members of the family, such as parents, brothers and sisters, or even new partners, especially where there are discussions concerning contact with the children of a divorcing couple.

Mediation is worth considering if you and your partner:

- Have argued yourselves to a standstill and need the intervention of an impartial third party.

- Feel that neutral ground as opposed to the kitchen table would be a better place to sort out your differences.

- Want to discover and discuss all the options for your own and your children's future.

- Want to know the options for housing.

- Need to know how the family assets can be divided.

Anything up to about six mediation sessions may be necessary, in the course of which you can explore your options and all their consequences. The mediator helps you examine your choices but doesn't make the decisions for you.

Once you and your ex have reached agreement, the mediator puts together a Memorandum of Understanding document which each party's solicitor can check for fairness. Then the document should be made legally binding by your solicitors so that you are both protected against any financial claims that may crop up in the future.

2 COLLABORATIVE LAW, which was introduced in 2005, could offer a solution if you want to avoid the acrimony and hassle that are the hallmarks of the average divorce, where each partner's respective solicitor slugs it out, usually in long and costly correspondence.

Basically, collaborative law is a way to get divorced with your dignity still intact and without running up enormous bills. Another notable benefit is the reduction in angst and trauma, so it minimises emotional fallout as well.

It involves the family lawyers and their clients on both sides agreeing in writing (in a document called a Participation Agreement) that they can reach a settlement without any court involvement. They undertake to meet and work together to resolve any contact and residence issues that have arisen, as well as the financial aspects and, if they need to, to call on the expertise of child specialists, tax advisers and others.

You remain in control throughout the process but your lawyer provides legal advice and guidance. Costs are kept down because correspondence between lawyers is discouraged and the process can be speeded up because there is no need to wait for court dates to be fixed before starting.

One of the salient features of the collaborative approach is that both lawyers have to withdraw from the case if the process breaks down, so that the clients have to find new lawyers and they may end up going down the adversarial route. Understandably, this encourages everyone concerned to come to an agreement.

The expert says...

"Conducting negotiations face-to-face, in an open and constructive way, benefits all members of the family. It is not just financially that most families emerge the better for this process. Parents and members of the wider family are often still able to get on in the aftermath of divorce. It is very much a question of trust – the sort of trust that can be eroded so quickly in family litigation."

Lawyer Roger Bamber, a partner and specialist in family
and matrimonial law with Mills & Reeve, Cambridge

Collaborative law may not be right for everyone, but it is worth looking at if you care about the following:

- You really don't want to fall out for ever with your partner or lose contact with their family.

- You are not intent on seeking revenge against your partner.

- You need your lawyer's help when negotiating in meetings with your partner.

- You prefer to have control over any changes to your arrangements for your children or your finances rather than leaving these up to the uncertainty of going to court.

Using your lawyer's skills in client representation, negotiation and problem-solving, you will be able to put together a fair agreement. Once this is in place, your lawyer will represent you in the divorce and prepare the court papers to obtain the consent order.

Solicitor Karina Leapman, who says her training in collaborative law was a life-changing experience, adds: "I am completely in favour of collaborative law. It's a wonderful solution that can be used, I suspect, in many cases. It is a different approach from mediation as clients have the support of their own solicitor throughout, and is, I think, a better way forward than the traditional adversarial system.

"How much better it is to avoid a court-led process which can harden attitudes and result in an outcome which is only 'all right', as opposed to the best possible outcome that the parties could have wished for themselves. I would like to see more cases dealt with in a less adversarial way."

Someone who chose the collaborative law procedure pays tribute to it in these words: " ... we can pay people to fight for each of us, or we can fight and pay people to referee, or we can work it out and pay people to help us. I'd rather do the last one!"

3 ONLINE DIVORCE enables you to obtain a divorce without spending time or money on a solicitor. Logging on could save you months and make the difference between being in the red or in the black at the end of it.

The use of divorce websites has grown in popularity along with the increase in use of the internet and is a serious option to consider if you don't have the added complications of financial and children issues.

There are plenty of online divorce sites offering 'value-for-money' services, costing from £65 plus the £340 court fee, so which one you choose is a matter for your own judgement – and, perhaps, personal recommendation.

The form-filling is all pretty straightforward (forms can be completed online or they can be sent to you by post) and it has the benefit of convenience too – a fact appreciated by one user who posted this grateful feedback on a divorce website: "As I have been unable to leave the house without being followed I would not otherwise have been able to start these proceedings."

Another commented: "I am very happy to report that this website has made an unhappy time far more manageable. My partner and I agreed to divorce and were first daunted by solicitors' advice. It all seemed odd that two consenting adults couldn't simply agree to separate without expensive legal fees."

One online divorce option is to pay a little extra for a completely 'managed' service, whereby all the forms are filled in for you and you will only be asked for your signature where and when necessary. You are given your own dedicated full-time professional divorce case manager who works out a timetable that will speed up the whole process. One site even offers a 100% no quibble guarantee, though it doesn't make it clear who might do the quibbling.

As an alternative to divorcing online you could contact your local county court for their DIY divorce pack. Do bear in mind though that the online and DIY route is *not* recommended if you answer Yes to any of these questions:

- Are any children involved?
- Is any property involved?
- Is significant money involved?
- Is one of you working and one not?
- Are any pensions involved?
- Is your divorce likely to be acrimonious?

One route to a best possible divorce

Bella and Steven found themselves contemplating divorce when their marriage of 11 years was on the rocks. Steven, an accountant, persuaded Bella to attend relationship counselling hoping she would see the error of her ways. Bella agreed, hoping that they would both gain insights into the reasons for the breakdown, enabling them to improve their relationship. What in fact happened was that they both realised, sadly, that neither of them was prepared to change to accommodate the other – they had simply grown too far apart over the years.

Bella was desperately unhappy in her marriage and knew she had to split, but was at a loss as to how to go about it. She felt drained by her job as a dental nurse as well as mother of a son and daughter, aged 5 and 7, and ground down by her unhappy marital situation with a domineering husband. She did not have the funds to appoint a solicitor, and was anyway loath to do so knowing that this could inflame relations between her and her husband.

On a friend's recommendation she consulted the Divorce Coach [*see below*]. The first session with the coach enabled her to clarify what it was that she needed: a strategy designed to obtain the best possible outcome for herself, while putting their children's needs foremost. For Bella, this meant separating with little blame attached to the other party or each other, and divorcing two years later. Before the second session with the coach, Bella consulted a solicitor who ran through what she might expect by way of a financial settlement and how best to make provision for their children.

In subsequent coaching sessions Bella was able to give vent to some of the worries she felt were adversely affecting the children, rather than let them spill over at home. She discussed with the coach how best to approach the issues she needed to address regarding her separation and how she might persuade her husband to attend family mediation sessions.

With the help of the coach and an independent financial adviser she compiled financial forms which calculated the family's net worth and their monthly expenditure, the sort of task she would hitherto have left to her husband. She began to see how the finances could be divided into two, even though her husband was telling her otherwise. When he put a ludicrous settlement to her, she was able to reject it, knowing that it did not represent the full picture.

After a further coaching session she was able to spell out the options to her husband: they go to court and spend money they didn't have on legal bills; they do nothing and soon one or other of them would crack up or leave home, also running the risk of the children being traumatised; or they both attend mediation. She was thus able to persuade her husband to try mediation. Because she had the family's financial figures to hand, she was able to follow what was being discussed and make useful contributions in support of her own case, despite some opposition from her husband.

After six sessions of mediation they were able to draw up an agreement before they physically parted. For Bella it represented a major breakthrough as it enabled her to see what compromises had to be made before they parted and how they expected the other to behave. But above all, she saw that they could successfully separate, something she could not previously have envisaged.

Steven now recognises that, armed with an agreement they are both committed to because they both contributed to it, they are more likely to retain a cordial relationship. As a good father he knows how important this is for his children's well-being.

"I am so glad now that Bella had divorce coaching from the beginning," he concedes. "To be honest, I would never have considered it, but it got us into mediation, where we were able to thrash out an agreement which wouldn't otherwise have been possible and it saved us money on legal fees."

(Thanks to Kirsten Gronning, the Divorce Coach, for this case study, in which names have been changed)

Divorce coaching

Kirsten Gronning is founder of The Divorce Coach based in Richmond, Surrey, where she sees clients one-to-one or coaches them over the phone or through e-courses via her website. She also runs a monthly self-help forum and workshops [*see box at end of chapter*].

There are divorce life coaches who help people get their life back on track after divorce, but Kirsten works with people before and through divorce, while they still have many options open to them.

"There is a growing need for divorce coaching," she says. "People are increasingly saying they want and need cheaper ways to divorce and I think that they will be looking at simpler, more cost-effective ways to get the best possible divorce. Divorce-related lawyers are starting to realise that they can't be the best people to deal with all aspects of divorce – especially with regard to the emotional and children issues – and that it is in everyone's interest that they take a more 'inter-disciplinary' approach to helping their clients through divorce.

"There is an unfulfilled need for clear support and guidance through serious relationship breakdown which isn't of a legal or financial nature (I try not to get involved in the finer details of either, but I do have a good legal understanding of the family law process and how the law treats the splitting of the finances, and it is here where I can really add value to the client and make their journey easier).

"I support people facing change due to separation and divorce by guiding them through the issues and situations facing them in order to achieve the best possible resolution with the minimum litigation where possible.

"It is not therapy but a cost-effective service [*starting from £110 a month*] which complements the help available from other professionals.

"When people approach me for help I find it is usually fear that is behind their emotional fall-out, coupled with feelings of loss, anger and sometimes guilt. The fear comes from not knowing what they are getting into and not knowing how they'll find the reserves – emotionally and financially – to get through.

"By helping the client see what the options are, we talk about what is achievable, within a time-frame, and work out small steps to achieve it. By this time they are already on the way to being able to get some clarity around their situation, which will empower them to move forward and I support them along the way, so that they increase in confidence and can see there is a brighter future around the corner.

"My message is simple: the more knowledge you have, the more powerful you are and the more that you know, the more you can take control and help yourself."

EXTRA HELP

- Resolution (formerly the Solicitors Family Law Association) is an association of solicitors who specialise in family law, including solicitors who specialise in cohabitation matters: 01689 820272 www.resolution.org.uk

- The Family Mediation Helpline can give general information on family mediation, advise you if your case is suitable for mediation and whether or not you may be eligible for public funding and help you find a family mediator in your locality. Helpline 0845 60 26 627 or go to www.familymediationhelpline.co.uk

- The website www.advicenow.org.uk/familymediation offers downloadable family mediation guides and podcasts.

- The National Family Mediation Service is a network of local not-for-profit family mediation services in England and Wales which helps couples, married or unmarried, going through separation and divorce: www.nfm.org.uk. For information about services in Scotland contact Family Mediation Scotland on 0845 119 2020 or via www.familymediationscotland.org.uk.

- The Institute of Family Therapy and Family Mediation Service, based in London, offers counselling and therapy for families and couples and children mediation service for separating and divorcing couples in joint sessions with a mediator or therapist. Call 020 7391 9150 or go to www.instituteoffamilytherapy.org.uk

- The Collaborative Family Law Group has a search facility for finding a local trained collaborative lawyer as well as a downloadable guide on its website: www.collablaw.org.uk

- The Collaborative Family Lawyers organisation, which has the slogan 'For better, not worse' has a directory of lawyers in collaborative practice on its website: www.collaborativefamilylawyers.co.uk

- One of the leading online divorce websites is www.divorce-online.co.uk or there's www.quickie-divorce.com or any number of others.

- For all aspects of relationship breakdown and its consequences, including advice on family law, try the site that does what it says in its title: www.divorceaid.co.uk

- Ondivorce has a legal advice helpline 0906 9060250 (calls cost £1.50 a minute) or you can go to: www.ondivorce.co.uk

- The website of the Simple Free Law Advisor aims to make the law easier for lay people to understand: www.sfla.co.uk

- Kirsten Gronning, the Divorce Coach: 0208 1239 046

www.divorcecoaching.co.uk and for online coaching:
http://divorcecoach.typepad.com/blog/2007/07/divorce-support.html

- Karina Leapman, collaborative lawyer: 020 7794 7741
  kl@karina-leapman.co.uk

CHAPTER 3

Riding the storm

You have to be tough to come through something like this. Most of the divorcees I have met have not suffered abuse as part of the break-up. It's just the usual shouting and screaming, which is relatively easy to deal with and there is just the hurt of losing a loved one. *Chris*

Much as you might wish to ride off into the sunset and pretend none of the past few months and years had ever happened, like it or not you're stuck. Sure, you may not be under the same roof as the person whose very presence has of late either caused you to weep or gnash your teeth – or both – but life is going to have to go on in much the same way as before. The irritation has gone. What has taken its place is the hard reality, and often the inescapable sadness, of life on your own. You're breathing the same air you used to breathe, just not for all the same reasons.

But life must go on – you have work to do, maybe mouths to feed, a mortgage or rent to pay. Out of all that's gone before, you have, let's hope, salvaged your pride and a determination to make life work for you. More than most, you need that most precious attribute: optimism.

It's not going to be easy to ride this storm on your own, but ride it you will. This chapter offers you the chance to learn how others have done it, through sometimes almost unendurable adversity, and to pick up some wise advice along the way.

Jane's story

Age at marriage: 26
Age at break-up: 39

Any children?

A son aged five

What was the cause of the split?

I had got married 'for ever' but looking back we were going in different directions. He left to find his own space. I later found out he was having an affair.

I just think we came from different backgrounds, and I think that has a bearing on relationships. I had had a difficult time as a child and looking back now I think this also had something to do with the difficulties we experienced. Perhaps I expected too much. He was not the person for me.

What efforts did you make individually or as a couple to save the marriage?

Communication between us became increasingly difficult but we thought some outside intervention might help.

If you turned to professionals, in what ways did they help?

We went to a counsellor. This was no help at all. My abiding picture of the woman is that she never took her coat off.

My solicitor was very supportive, but at the time everything is being thrown at you and perhaps decisions are made that in hindsight are wrong.

Every case is different. Perhaps I should have given the situation more thought, but I had been left with a small child and I just wanted to get on with life if my husband didn't want us.

How did you sort out the financial and residence issues?

This was certainly not easy. There were four court cases in all. I still get angry thinking about it.

Perhaps it is best summed up by the fact that I received several sheets of paper with my husband's requests for contents of the house, down to half the light bulbs!

My son had been offered a place as a chorister at a school. During one of the court cases his father said he didn't approve of private education. I can remember saying "Then I'll educate him myself," which I did, but that's another story.

He has not seen his father for years. I asked him not long ago "What would you say if I told you Dad had died?" He replied: "Why? Has he?"

How were you affected, emotionally and physically, by the split?

I really don't know how I was affected emotionally. I felt shell-shocked but I had watched my mother in a difficult situation bringing up me and my brother almost single-handedly. My father was an alcoholic so I suppose I somehow looked at the situation as the norm. I thought 'I'll just do it myself'.

Unfortunately, I developed a tumour which required extensive surgery. There is a school of thought that such situations can be accelerated by shock.

How did you cope when you were living alone?

Unless you have been in the situation you do not know what life could possibly be like. With the best of intentions people may say they understand, but every situation is different and therefore requires different handling.

I have just kept smiling and got on with life. I took a full-time job, because I had to, but even if I hadn't needed to it was necessary in order to become a person in my own right.

Would you have done anything differently?

I know I should have dealt with my finances in a different way, and saved some money.

How long did it take to put your life back together, or at least to feel like facing the world?

Perhaps I am still doing it 20 years on, I don't know. I am still angry – I think. I have just got on with life although in lots of ways it hasn't been easy, especially financially and emotionally.

How has your life evolved since the break-up?

I went straight into a full-time job to support myself and my son. I have had a totally different life being divorced. I think I have achieved lots of things I wouldn't have had the opportunity to take on had I remained married.

I certainly could not have coped without my friends. I must have driven them mad at times!

There is a 'but' in all of this: I think there is an art to being single or divorced. You have to know when to be on your own and how to cope with the situation.

Any advice for others?

- Remember you are a person with a life and this is not a rehearsal.

- Keep smiling.

David's story

Age at marriage: 27
Age at break-up: 52

Any children?
Four daughters aged 23, 21 and twins of 19

What was the cause of the split?
My wife arranged a school reunion through Friends Reunited and ran off with a boyfriend she'd had at school.

What efforts did you make individually or as a couple to save the relationship?
I begged her to reconsider but there was no stopping her. It was as though someone had taken over her mind.

If you turned to professionals, in what ways did they help?
No therapists or anything like that – my wife was not interested.

How did you sort out the finances?
Perhaps surprisingly, the financial settlement was amicable with minimal expense.

How were you affected, emotionally and physically, by the split?
I was very affected emotionally. It affected my work big time

(I'm a builder). I felt inadequate and did not want to see clients about work. I drove my friends mad by talking about it.

How did you cope when you were living alone?

I was competent with cooking but I forgot to pay bills. I felt very lonely – and alone.

Would you have done anything differently?

I don't think so. I was a good provider and a good father. As for my relationship, I suppose we might have lost ourselves at some time, as we were both busy working to keep a household and four children going.

How long did it take to put your life back together, or at least to feel like facing the world?

It took me a while to get over my split. Two things that helped me a lot were building my own house and creating a website: www.been-dumped.com.

I never held a grudge or showed contempt because I'm not that kind of person. I was just very sad that the woman I thought that I knew for 25 years could behave this way.

How has your life evolved since the break-up?

I have slowly got myself back on track with the help of my children and Paul, one of my future sons-in-law, who works with me and who was there for me while I was at my lowest. He and two other friends, Brett and Neil, helped me create been-dumped.com. I wanted to do this because I needed to find and help people in my situation as you experience feelings that you couldn't explain to anyone who hasn't been there.

After a year I thought I'd fallen in love again with a lady I met through been-dumped.com. But it was too soon for her after her split and too soon for me so I got hurt there, but it helped me to get over my wife. Now four years have passed and I'm back on track again.

I don't know whether I wish to have a relationship again or not. Once bitten twice shy, as they say!

Any advice for others?

- Make friends by joining a club of some sort.

- Don't watch any sad programmes on TV.

- Have a glass of wine, but don't drink too much as it will prolong the recovery process and make you depressed for longer.

- Find things to do in the house like changing things around a bit to make it different.

- Join www.been-dumped.com – it helped me enormously. I have lots of emails from members to prove how much it has helped them, too.

The expert says...

The relationship charity Relate warns that websites such as Friends Reunited, which can bring old flames from schooldays back together, along with dating websites and new technology such as mobile phones, have made infidelity increasingly easy.

Relate counsellor Paula Hall says: "People are living longer, healthier lives. Someone in their 50s who is in an unhappy relationship would face a further 30 or 40 active years with the wrong partner. Many women (and men) are realising they just don't want to spend that much time with a partner they no longer love."

Chris's story

Age at marriage: 48
Age at break-up: 50

Any children?

Two step-daughters aged 16 and 14

What was the cause of the split?

My wife had an affair. I instigated the divorce because I found out about the affair and I could not take her back.

What efforts did you make individually or as a couple to save the marriage?

None. For me it was over. I take fidelity as very important in a marriage and once my partner cheated on me there was no going back.

If you turned to professionals, in what ways did they help?

I was sent to Relate. She didn't want to go but she said I had to go because I had a problem. However, the only thing counselling did was make me realise I didn't have a problem.

My solicitor is doing OK at the moment, but as the divorce is ongoing we will see. The signs are good.

How did you sort out the finances?

She dictated what she wanted and I was told that if I didn't go along with that she would make things very hard for me. She and her boyfriend marched me down to a solicitor and I was asked to sign some documents. It was made plain to me that failure to do so would result in me not getting the mortgage for my new home. The divorce is still going through so we're awaiting the financial outcome.

She did everything she could do to turn the children against me. I don't see them any more. The children seemed to want the split. They actively encouraged the abuse and revelled in it when it was dished out. They turned into cruel, vicious monsters. For weeks on end I was regularly kept awake night after night, until the early hours of the morning, by them taking it in turns to shout and scream at me and try and break me down. I would just sit there. I would look at the clock and yawn and my youngest would say: "Why don't you f*** off to bed, you bastard?" My youngest was the most vicious but it was a free-for-all and their mother and her boyfriend joined in too.

How were you affected, emotionally and physically, by the split?

I was affected very badly by what happened to me. The affair was neither here nor there. It happened and I got over that and decided to move on. My wife took umbrage at this and set about getting some kind of revenge on me for daring to leave her. She also wanted her boyfriend to be the new dad. So she did some very bad things to me to achieve this.

It's five months now since I left. I am nowhere near over it. The nightmares are gone now but I still get the flashbacks. I have weird physical side-effects. My hands go all tingly and I get slightly breathless. I get a little light-headed. Certain sounds also give me flashbacks. But it is getting better. I know I will get over it.

How did you cope when you were living alone?

About two months into the worst year of my life I sat down with a load of Diazepam and Amitriptlyne. There was definitely enough to kill me several times over. Something stopped me. Something told me that I would survive and be OK. I don't know what it was or how, but I just knew.

My sister has been a great help to me. She was my only friend when I had no one. Since I left I have met my current partner. She has also helped me. Mostly this has come from me. I battle with it day by day, taking every opportunity to tell myself how lucky I am. It could have been far worse. I got away relatively unscathed.

Would you have done anything differently?

I should have looked at the signs. I am in part to blame for what happened to me. I should never have married her. I should have looked into her past and what she did to her previous husband and how he was dispatched. But I didn't. That I have to live with.

How long did it take to put your life back together, or at least to feel like facing the world?

I am not over it but I am getting there. I have been in my new property for five months and I am slowly recovering. Undoing what they did will take some time but I am determined to rebuild my life.

How has your life evolved since the break-up?

You have to be tough to come through something like this. Most of the divorcees I have met have not suffered abuse as part of the break-up. It's just the usual shouting and screaming, which is relatively easy to deal with and there is just the hurt of losing a loved one.

I was lucky (or unlucky – it depends on where you stand) to have been physically abused as a child so I was sort of prepared to cope with the emotional pain. But my parents never did this kind of thing to me. This was far worse than I have ever had.

It was the toughest 11 months of my life. I don't think there is any help that can be given. It's up to the individual to survive as best they can. Some do and some don't.

Any advice for others?

- Tough it out.

- Plan, plan and plan.

- Just stick in there and believe in your ability to withstand whatever is thrown at you.

- Always remember: things will get better.

Dawn's story

Age at start of relationship: 17
Age at break-up: 27

Any children?

Daughter, aged one at the time

What was the cause of the split?

Our constant arguing made it impossible for us to go on living together. I broke up the relationship because I felt I had outgrown it, even though we'd just had a child.

What efforts did you make individually or as a couple to save the marriage?

To be honest, I felt as though I had spent the past 10 years trying to save the relationship – it was doomed from the start. It was when our daughter was born that I realised how we could never be a proper couple, however hard we tried, and splitting up was the best thing to do.

If you turned to professionals, in what ways did they help?

Neither of us felt we needed help from outsiders – although we did have three visits from the police due to my partner's aggressive behaviour.

How did you sort out the financial and residence issues?

There was nothing to sort out financially and as far as residence was concerned, my daughter stayed with me.

We had a housing association property so just transferred it to my name and I have carried on living there ever since. I have always provided for my daughter and to this day I have never received any financial support from her father. However, on a positive note, his family make up for his shortcomings.

How were you affected, emotionally and physically, by the split?

The split was not pleasant – are they ever? My only concern was for my daughter and how she might be affected. Eight years on, I can safely say she is a well-balanced child who sees her father and his family on a regular basis.

How did you cope when you were living alone again?

Our daughter was too young at the time to know what was going on, but I firmly believe that she would have been badly affected by the rows and fighting had her father and I stayed together.

Would you have done anything differently?

I wish I had urged my partner to seek help before things got into such a mess. I still would have left him as we had grown apart, but I feel his life would be much better now if he had got help at the time.

How long did it take to put your life back together, or at least to feel like facing the world?

Luckily I was surrounded by great friends and an amazing family, so my recovery was quick, but it was my daughter's needs that always kept me focused.

Having her to care for helped me get over any feelings of loneliness I may have had, so I recovered quite quickly. But I was full of hate for my ex-partner for a long time. In fact I still hate him now, on occasions.

How has your life evolved since the break-up?

The incredibly close relationship I enjoy with my daughter and the amazing life we have together just makes me stronger and stronger.

What were the most important steps you took?

Once I'd made the decision to split up, I stuck to it and I stayed positive. I had always thought that if children are involved you should do everything in your power to keep the family together. I no longer believe this as the environment we lived in back then was not a good one (there were drugs and drink involved). While being alone with a small child can be very scary and sometimes very lonely, it was the best decision I've ever made.

Any advice for others?

- Believe in yourself.
- Remember that life really is wonderful.

THE 'COMMON LAW' MYTH

David Allison, representing the family law group Resolution, welcomes proposals from the Law Commission to make the law fairer for couples who live together and give them some legal protection.

Under the existing law, many people who choose to live with someone and not marry may suffer significant injustice and financial hardship if their relationship breaks down, or if their partner dies. Most unmarried couples don't know or understand their lack of protection or rights – most believe, wrongly, that they are protected by the so-called status of 'common law' husband or wife and only find out that this is a myth when things go wrong.

"What is being proposed," David says, "is a safety net provision for people who have suffered an economic disadvantage because of the relationship. For example, if a partner gives up work to care for children and as a consequence has no capital, income or pension provision, and if the relationship breaks down many years later she will, under these proposals, be able to make a financial claim.

"In the absence of any laws to protect cohabitants, there is no provision for a judge to take these factors into account and arrive at fair solutions which recognise the contributions of both people in a relationship. These proposals will prevent unmarried women from coming out of the relationship with nothing, as they often do at the moment."

George's story

Age at start of relationship: 20
Age at break-up: 33

Any children?
Aged 12 and two

What was the cause of the split?
It was brought about by my partner's health problems that led

to prescription drug abuse and addiction. Her health problems had started with post-natal depression and migraines and developed from there.

What efforts did you make individually or as a couple to save the marriage?

I changed my occupation so that I could spend more time at home.

If you turned to professionals, in what ways did they help?

My partner consulted a psychiatrist on the recommendation of our family doctor, but unfortunately the situation went from bad to worse. She abused the drugs she was prescribed and was totally addicted to anti-depressants and codeine.

How did you sort out the financial and residence issues?

We sold the home and split the profit. It was pretty simple – just a separation agreement at the time. She was not mentally capable of looking after the children so they stayed with me.

The oldest child witnessed the turmoil and his mother's condition even though we tried to keep his life as normal as possible. I think he felt that I had abandoned his mother but in later years came to understand that we tried to keep the relationship together.

How were you affected, emotionally and physically, by the split?

I suffered a great feeling of failure regarding the relationship and the children.

After so many years of dealing with the medical profession and various doctors I was physically and emotionally exhausted. I realised that I had a responsibility for my own life and needed to change the environment for the children. I felt that the children's emotional needs were being neglected because the focus was always on their mother.

The dream of a well-adjusted happy family remained just a dream. The reality is that a family does not have to have both a mother and father. There are well-adjusted families in which there is only one adult, where one partner has died, say. In my case I felt that the split was like a death. I had no ill feelings towards my partner, just a great contempt for the medical profession who were unable to help and who I believe were the major cause of her health problems and, in due course, our break-up.

How did you cope when you were living alone?

As soon as I was on my own with the kids it was like a great weight had been lifted from me. I felt that I had a life again.

A single father with two kids was not that common where we lived and when I would take the kids out to the park or things like that I was always among mums with their kids. At first I was worried they might think I was a child molester because normally in the middle of the day the father should be at work and not at the park with kids.

Would you have done anything differently?

I regret that we had to seek professional help for my partner's health concerns and depression. I very strongly feel that they were the cause of her addiction, which led to the split.

How long did it take to put your life back together, or at least to feel like facing the world?

About a year after the split I was lucky enough to meet the woman who was instrumental in helping me put my life back together again.

How has your life evolved since the break-up?

My life revolved around the kids and then I met a woman who made me realise that I had a responsibility to myself as well. She helped me to understand that I could be a responsible father and still have a life. After a very long time I was able to enjoy my life as an adult again, especially once I'd managed to rid myself of the feelings of guilt.

Any advice for others?

- Take responsibility for yourself.

- Don't take as long as I did to finally make a decision.

- Do not put all your faith in the medical profession. Trust your gut feelings probably more so than the professionals.

Vicky's story

Age at marriage: 23
Age at break-up: 49

Any children?
Four: aged 25, 22, 18 and 14

What was the cause of the split?
My husband decided to leave. He was in a relationship with someone else.

What efforts did you make individually or as a couple to save the marriage?
I tried to talk it through with him but he had decided not to discuss the matter. He was set on leaving and nothing I could say would change his mind.

If you turned to professionals, in what ways did they help?

I went to Relate (he wouldn't go) but it did no good in the end. I think it probably made me look at the relationship more objectively and take an outsider's view of the partnership – and this in turn made me realise how I had failed to take this on board.

How did you sort out the financial and residence issues?

It all seemed very long and drawn out but compared with most it probably wasn't. It took about two-and-a-half years from the time of first seeing a solicitor to the time of the decree absolute coming through. Our home had to be sold and I bought a much more modest place nearby where I started life again on my own. The children were all old enough to decide what they wanted and they continued to see their father occasionally. Because there were four of them the impact of their loss was shared – it brought them all closer together as a unit to deal with this new situation.

How were you affected, emotionally and physically, by the split?

Because of my husband's alcohol dependency all trust had broken down; behaviour was unpredictable and unreliable. The relationship had been deteriorating over a number of years. When eventually the split came there was some relief that I would no longer have to try and improve this – but huge disappointment that all my efforts to save the marriage had failed. I believed I had fought a long time for this.

Initially I felt huge disappointment that his feelings for his children were not strong enough to keep the family together. I also felt great resentment that another woman – who also happened to be the godmother of one of my children – was happy to foster this relationship with a man who had responsibilities to a wife and four children (how old-fashioned can you get?).

There was a huge sense of failure, too, that I had failed to keep my man, or create a successful relationship, or provide my children with a happy family background, and a great feeling that I had let everybody down.

Significantly, there was also a big sense of loss – of status as a married woman and loss of a companion, although this had been lost before the split. He was living away from home in the week and becoming less and less communicative when he returned at weekends. There was also the loss of support from a fellow parent, although we'd moved around a lot as a family and because of my husband working away from home so much and not being exactly a hands-on type of father, I was not unfamiliar with the single parent role

There was and still is a big sense of loneliness. The world of single women is not one I really want to inhabit. They are seen by some couples as a threat, by men as other men's cast-offs, as though there must be something wrong with them, and a bit sad as having failed to attract a new man in their life. I have many single friends in my situation and we all wonder where all the single men are.

On the positive side there was a great feeling of freedom and independence, which I still relish. I am not exactly a born housewife and, unlike some friends I know in similar situations, do not miss having to look after a man. I do believe some women are born to run a home and minister to a mate and so the single state is probably much harder for them.

Physically, apart from the impact of the emotional upheaval, I didn't suffer any particular problems.

How did you cope when you were living alone?

I tried very hard not to feel bitter. I thought that he may have mucked up my marriage but I wasn't going to let him muck up the rest of my life. I have things to offer – I need to be a functioning parent for my children – and so screwing myself up with resentment was not going to help.

You need to do a stock-taking exercise to establish what strengths are available and what you are hoping to achieve with the rest of your life. Knowing that there wouldn't be much cash around, I remember working out that, having established a home, apart from my family, my future day-to-day happiness would come from my friendships and the joy I gained from my garden, watching birds and wildlife and exploring the countryside, all of which need cost nothing.

Would you have done anything differently?

I believe good communication is the key to a good relationship. I did not know nearly enough about this or how to create it – and also I married a man who did not want to communicate. Perhaps we should all have lessons in communication skills.

Also, alcohol played a large part in the breakdown of our relationship. If I had known more about alcoholism I might have done many things differently.

How long did it take to put your life back together, or at least to feel like facing the world?

Slowly, slowly life adjusted to a more even keel – ten years on I was probably more or less readjusted.

As time went by I realised I had to put the whole thing behind me, learn from it and create a new life. I still feel a huge sense of failure but no longer have any bitter feelings – just contempt for myself, maybe, for letting it happen.

I have one friend who is still blaming her ex for walking out on her ten years ago. She still believes he has wrecked her life and she has tried to poison her children's minds with verbal attacks on their father. The result is that the split still dominates her life and it is hard for her to achieve any contentment in her single state.

I personally found it much easier once my ex had died, four years after the divorce. It left a gap but ended any conflict for the children and created a new sense of freedom from the past. I'm not suggesting murder as a solution, but his death did bring an end to a very unhappy chapter.

How has your life evolved since the break-up?

I have gradually, over the years, established myself in a single state. Meeting people who did not know me as a married woman went some way towards creating this new single identity. Studying for a degree helped me to think things through and give myself a new qualification.

As for putting myself back on my feet, time is a great help, friends are extremely important and I personally feel that I was supported by a flickering faith in God.

My upbringing of stiff upper lip, responsibility, duty and all those sort of things kept me functioning as a mother and I also wanted to be as much help as I could to my children as they adjusted to the upheaval in their lives.

Any advice for others?

- Try and arrive at a state of mind when the past can be left behind and you can start to look ahead. That is definitely a positive step.

- Find solace and support among others in the same situation.

Through Sally Moon's Old Bags' Club (now defunct) I was put in touch with four other women in the area who had been ditched. We all found it helpful to realise we were not alone and took strength from sharing our experiences.

REVENGE

Lady Sally Graham-Moon briefly became a heroine figure for dumped wives when she exacted revenge on her errant husband by chopping a sleeve off each of his 32 Savile Row suits, pouring white paint over his BMW while it was outside his mistress's house, and distributing the expensive contents of his wine cellar on neighbours' doorsteps. She founded the Old Bags' Club to give support to deserted wives and it, and she, were widely publicised. The club disbanded two years later, in 1994.

There have been many high-profile cases of revenge over the years. While they may provoke mirth they also have a certain poignancy, not least because those involved are tormented and are driven to desperate measures. A Pembrokeshire guesthouse owner, for example, who found his wife in bed with a guest, took his revenge by throwing the man's clothes into a septic tank.

Other victims of their spouse's infidelity have resorted to telling the world about it as a means of revenge. This was the course chosen by a woman in Birmingham who emptied their joint account to pay for a giant advertising hoarding proclaiming her husband's deceit with one of her best friends.

Then there was Pavla, the wronged wife of the Czech prime minister, Mirek Topolanek, who hit upon a novel way of getting her own back: she ran for a rival political party.

An angry Welshman, hurt by his ex-wife taking up with his best friend, put revealing pictures of her up for sale on the internet auction site eBay. He compiled CDs, each containing 200 images of her, and sold them at £4.99 a pop. There were plenty of takers, apparently.

Italians in the town of Rocca Canterano, 45km east of Rome, have an interesting take on infidelity: they hold a festa to celebrate betrayed spouses all over the world. Each November, the Festa del Cornuto features floats bearing costumed actors who recite satirical verse and prose specially written for the unfortunate victims of infidelity past and present. It being Italy, where they need little excuse for a hooley, the day-long event also features food, singing, dancing and a great deal of merrymaking.

The expert says...

There will always be those for whom revenge is a preferred way of releasing negative emotions. Publicly damaging their (ex) partner's property or publicly telling 'their story' in the aftermath of the public split are two examples, but the longer campaigns of bitterness and revenge which are played out for years, often through the courts and through the children, are another example.

As a 'coping strategy' does it work? It may release pent-up feelings which may otherwise show up elsewhere, but where does it lead? A client came to me when her marriage to a well-known man ended when he publicly cheated on her. Was she tempted to tell reporters? Yes. Did she? No. Her aim was to move on and she understood that wreaking revenge wouldn't allow her to move on.

If there's any doubt I'd recommend asking whether, by taking the action of revenge, you'd be moving towards your desire to put the separation in the past or away from it.

If my client had publicly lambasted her ex-husband, how would it have made her feel? Perhaps powerful for a short time, glad to have got it off her chest. But how would her children have felt; how might her spouse have retaliated and what damage might it ultimately have done to her desire to reach a financial settlement at least cost?

Awareness of the reason for your feelings is the first step to gaining control of them, and letting go of them. Revenge is an emotional response to fear, anger, loss and sometimes guilt. Accept your feelings and find constructive ways of facing up to what they mean through support groups, reading personal growth books and counselling and coaching. Aim to put the past behind you and live in the present. Plan your future by making and embracing change, rather than by taking out your frustrations and disappointments on your (ex) partner. It will never be fair and you will never get even.

Kirsten Gronning, the Divorce Coach

Thisbe's story

Age at marriage: 21
Age at break-up: 50

Any children?

Two: a daughter aged 25 and just married, a son aged 24 and working away from home

What was the cause of the split?

Our separation was largely due to generational patterning and of course our parents' behaviour was generational in their turn. 'Pyramus' and I had both been brought up in emotionally unreliable, artistic milieus. While this encouraged our creativity and unconventionality, our need for stability and demonstrative loving had been somewhat neglected.

As is often the case, our immediate attraction was, in all likelihood, the subconscious recognition of parental characteristics and lifestyles. Pyramus and I both had tempestuous and unfaithful artist fathers. His father and mother, who were not married, had repeated affairs, but my mother was faithful and forbearing with her errant husband and provided him and me with an ostensibly solid family home, even though it lacked real warmth.

I quickly realised that underneath the glamorous personality that Pyramus had inherited he longed for security and emotional stability. He told me that he didn't love me, but we had both learnt to be wary of romantic love and agreed that friendship was a more trustworthy basis for marriage. I believed that if I followed my mother's example true love would grow between us. Our parents approved the match to the extent that it was almost decided by them. Deeper discussion was not risked and we just trusted to our instincts.

We married very swiftly. In the 1960s to be unmarried was to be seen as a failure. My upbringing had left me with low self-esteem and I was relieved that someone would actually want me, especially someone handsome and dynamic. In my case the wedding was a typical case of 'aisle, altar, hymn' – always a mistake, but for a while it worked.

Soon after our large wedding Pyramus was violent to me. I was shocked but excused it as being the result of his insecurity. Having been told that one has to work at marriage, I also saw it as a failure on my part.

Gradually, as Pyramus came to trust me, the violence stopped but, unfortunately, although I didn't realise it consciously, my loving response to him had become permanently frozen, replaced by fear and a lack of respect. Nevertheless we worked well as a team, linked by our interest in our two children, our home making (literally restoring houses) and our creative jobs. To a large extent our marriage was a good one. It was certainly seen as such by others who flocked to our hospitality. After a while, however, we slept apart.

When the children were teenagers, quite naturally challenging their parents' authority and having their own love affairs, the violence returned. However, it still didn't occur to me to leave Pyramus. Through needy vulnerability, I fell in love for the first time, but not with him. Our divorce finally came about through a practicality. We were asked to renew a long lease with our tenants and both admitted that we could not sign it because the marriage had long been over.

What efforts did you make individually or as a couple, to save the marriage?

From the start I had tried making advances towards Pyramus, but I had always been repulsed as he had to take the lead in all things. Discussions were dangerous as they were seen as arguments and risked his wrath and worse. As we had married without testing the relationship, once the divorce was decided we made no effort to save the marriage.

If you turned to professionals in what ways did they help?

Our way of coping with divorce was to present a friendly unity to our children and to outsiders. We were determined to confuse the scandal-mongers who scavenge on misfortune, so we continued to go out together in public. We agreed that our parental solidarity was even more important than any new relationships that might ensue and we have succeeded in retaining this attitude.

To our surprise, our solicitors assumed that we would be hostile towards each other, but we proved that it was otherwise and sorted our affairs swiftly on an equally divided basis. A friend who is a therapist supported me in my view that the loving is in the letting go but I believe that Pyramus went forward without addressing his feelings.

How did you sort out the finances?

Pyramus had taken total charge of the finances and after divorcing I was ill-equipped to understand them. A prey to financial advisers, I made decisions that I now regret. I was too ashamed to admit that I didn't understand the terms used, or the forms that I signed.

How were you affected emotionally and physically by the split?

I felt relief that I was free but was afraid of coping alone. It was assumed that I would quickly find a new husband, but it seems to be the case that men find partners more easily. Pyramus was treated with sympathy, while I was surprised to find myself seen as predatory and damaged.

People clearly feared that I would burden them with my problems, so I worked overly at appearing cheerful and strong. I didn't miss Pyramus at all as I knew that I had retained the best of what we had and provided sufficient emotional and financial security for the children.

Pyramus swiftly found a new wife and, although she was conventionally hostile to me to begin with, she soon realised that this was an unnecessary and unwelcome attitude. The children were helpful in assuring her that I was no threat. I am aggrieved, however, to be treated by Pyramus and his wife as guilty when in fact I had done my best and had had every reason to escape the marriage. I believe that Pyramus has not acknowledged his part in causing our separation.

How did you cope when you were living alone?

I set out to make full use of my talents and to be self-sufficient; I was nevertheless hoping to find the companionship, tenderness and protection of a partner. Instead, reflecting my own pain, I attracted needy, unsuitable men and ended up alone. I have found that other single ladies are often rather embittered, spurning men and marriage and scorning sex, so I keep my diminishing hope of a partner rather quiet. It has to be said that there is much pleasure in autonomy and privacy, but there is also loneliness. Being a grandmother is a comfort and joy, but one has to accept a background role.

Would you have done anything differently?

I don't think I could have done. I don't regret my marriage or the divorce, but I regret the damage it did to my son, who is the real casualty. Unlike my daughter he didn't understand the problems with the marriage and blamed me for the divorce. He now has commitment problems but I dearly hope that he will find happiness in time.

How long did it take to put your life back together or at least to feel like facing the world?

Immediately. Not yet. Probably never! I just don't know.

How has your life evolved since the break-up?

The contrasts of my life remain the same. I am more and more fulfilled as a working artist and writer, socially active and a busy grandmother – but still lonely. Achieving one's 'inner marriage' as one is told one must before having hope of an outer marriage, seems impossible and indeed incomprehensible.

Any advice for others?

- Accept your faults and understand your partner's.

- Remember that nobody owns another. Loving is in the letting go, and if you let people fly free they are more likely to fly back to you.

- Retain the best aspects of your relationship after divorce. Keep in contact for the sake of your children and don't play tug-of-war with them.

- Observe good manners.

- Cherish your friends. They may be lonely too. Assure them that they can retain friendships with both you and your ex-partner.

- Keep optimistic – life is full of surprises.

- Take care of yourself.

Taking the blame ...

In both these preceding case studies Thisbe and Vicky burden themselves and impede their recovery by accepting an unnecessary amount of the blame for the break-up of their respective marriages. Thisbe says she saw her husband's violence towards her as "a failure" on her part because it showed she hadn't worked at her marriage, yet she does concede that she did her best and had had "every reason to escape the marriage".

Vicky's self-recrimination is evident in her admission that, ten years on: "I still feel a huge sense of failure ... contempt for myself for letting it happen." And this breast-beating is from someone whose husband abandoned her for a case of whisky and the company of one of her friends.

Renouncing feelings of guilt, especially when they are unfounded like this, is the only way to move forward or life will forever be clouded. It is difficult to love yourself and all that makes you the person you are if there's a little part of you that feels unworthy and bad.

... and living with loneliness

Thisbe and Vicky also have in common their dislike of the unmarried state but feel they have no means of solving their problem. Where are all the single men, Vicky wonders, wistfully. "The world of single women is not one I really want to inhabit," she adds. After some unsatisfactory encounters Thisbe says, with immense poignancy: "I keep my diminishing hope of a partner rather quiet."

It is well-known that women in their situation are looked upon by other women as slightly dangerous predators and by men as someone else's sad cast-offs. This unkind stereotyping is cruel and unfair for, while it is perceived that divorced women generally have a harder time of it than divorced men in finding new partners, it is hard to escape the fact that the vast majority of suddenly-single women do remarry and enjoy happiness again. And those who don't marry probably share their life with a partner or at least have close and fulfilling friendships.

How to reach that state from the one of sad resignation endured by Thisbe and Vicky is explained in Chapter 7.

Tony's story

Age at marriage: 24
Age at break-up: 29

Any children?

Two, aged three and 18 months

What was the cause of the split?

It was apparently our incompatibility, which she perceived and I didn't. Not long after we separated it became clear to me (somewhat after other people) that my wife married me for security and for a family rather than for love. It is fair to say she may not have realised this herself and simply hoped, in vain, that children would cement the relationship, She had a short-lived affair after we split up, and eventually left our daughter and son with me to bring up, mainly because I had a loving family to support me, which she did not.

What efforts did you make individually or as a couple to save the marriage?

We talked a lot, round and round the problems without getting anywhere. I don't believe either of us at the time knew what was really wrong.

If you turned to professionals, in what ways did they help?

We visited Relate, just the once, to no avail, probably through no fault of theirs. Because we, or certainly I, hadn't a clue what was really at the root of our problems, they had little to go on.

My solicitor, who I knew well, was very supportive and he felt I should have custody of the children.

How did you sort out the financial and residence issues?

I kept the family home as I had the children with me. Later I was granted custody by the courts. It was lengthy and involved legal aid. My wife offered no opposition to custody but demanded more access than I was prepared to give and the courts agreed with me.

My son developed what was called emotional asthma and displayed an aggressive streak, which fortunately did not last too long as he began judo as a means of controlling it. Within a year or so he was back to his quiet and controlled self. My daughter seemed to take on the role of woman of the house and looked after her brother. They were both clingy with me and my family and needed lots of reassurance and affection.

Relations with their mother continued to be strained for many years and even now they are not as close as normal. They were affected but they have since said it helped having one parent always there and a loving family supporting them. Access weekends were disturbing for everyone concerned.

How were you affected, emotionally and physically, by the split?

I was devastated, hurt and very worried for the future because I knew the children weren't happy and wanted to live in their own home rather than in a flat with their mother far away. I lost a lot of weight and didn't really know what to do for the best. I concentrated on my job as best I could to take my mind off things.

How did you cope when you were living alone?

After the separation I had to decide how to look after the children and do my job and keep the home going. I decided to get a live-in nanny and went to an agency specialising in substitute mothers who come with children of their own and run your house and help bring up your children. This came about after six months or so and in a way it took my mind off the separation because there were now two other children and their mother to consider.

However, for all of us the first year or so of this new arrangement was an emotional roller-coaster, and not just because of the access weekends going in two different directions. A great group of loyal and supportive friends, plus my family, got me through this and everything that had gone before.

Would you have done anything differently?

Probably not, because the reasons for the break-up only became clear later on. Anyway, we both survived it and I have two wonderful children of my own that I would not have had otherwise.

How long did it take to put your life back together, or at least to feel like facing the world?

Probably 18 months or so. I worked hard at setting up a family unit to create some sort of normality and security for everyone concerned.

How has your life evolved since the break-up?

Against all my expectations, because I'd decided I probably wasn't suited to marriage after the first experience, I ended up marrying our live-in nanny. I have adopted her two children, who are similar in age to my own. It has helped give me back my confidence and I am glad to be able to create a proper family unit again for my daughter and son.

No one is more surprised than I am, but it's working out fine and I'm happy.

Any advice for others?

- It is important to go with your heart and your instincts.

- Good friends will still be there for you if you cock it up and make the wrong decision.

- Put your children first and give them security, safety and stability.

- Do not condemn the other parent in the presence of the children.

Shaun's story

Age at marriage: 32
Age at break-up: 38

Any children?

Three: aged seven, four and 18 months

What was the cause of the split?

My wife says that she no longer loves me. Money is also a problem. We had financial difficulties that I kept from her, which was a mistake – a big, huge, bloody mistake!

What efforts did you make individually or as a couple to save the marriage?

I have tried everything. She is no longer interested. I would give anything to get her back.

If you turned to professionals, in what ways did they help?

I have seen a counsellor who was more of a life coach really. She helped but not as much as a clairvoyant that I saw. She gave me an understanding of what was going off and that I would come through it a better person.

How did you sort out the financial and residence issues?

It is all ongoing, but so far it is amicable so hopefully we will reach agreements on these things that will be acceptable to both of us. It's been difficult for the children. I used to spend all my time with them, rushing home from work, feeding them, bathing them and putting them to bed. They are too young to realise what's happened. My four-year-old was a little subdued for a while but they seem all right now. I hope so anyway.

How were you affected, emotionally and physically, by the split?

Devastated. Drinking, smoking, not eating. Thinking of ending it all on more than a couple of occasions. Deep shock, anger, resentment, feeling lost. Not being able to understand why.

How did you cope when you were living alone again?

I don't like being on my own. I didn't eat properly for the first six or seven weeks. What's the point in cooking for yourself? I can run a house OK as I have always done the chores, the washing and ironing and so on.

Would you have done anything differently?

I would have been more honest about money. I would also have stood up for myself more and instead of buying something I'd have said "Look, things are tight, we need to wait a while".

How long did it take for you to get your life back together, or at least to feel like facing the world?

Maybe a couple of months. It's not been easy at all. I don't think I am out of the woods yet. I have good days and bad days. I'm dreading my wedding anniversary, then it'll be my four-year-old's birthday. I will just have to be strong.

How has your life evolved since the break-up?

I have had support from work colleagues but my family have been rubbish. The clairvoyant has really given me something to focus on. I really don't know how I'm getting through, but an inner strength seems to kick in – eventually.

Any advice for others?

- Talk to everyone and anyone about how you feel. It's not easy to talk and it is upsetting, but you have to have the belief that you will come through the other side.

- Get help.

- Don't be on your own.

- Don't drink too much.

- Don't keep contacting the other party. Don't smother them. If they love you then they will realise and make the first move back.

A few weeks week after completing his questionnaire, Shaun emailed to say: "Just to let you know that today I received the divorce papers from the court. I was dreading receiving them but when I opened them it didn't bother me at all. I even felt quite happy.

"It makes no sense at all to me but possibly this means that it's all over. I keep telling myself that I still love her but now I don't think I do any more. Sure, I'm sad that the marriage is over but it feels like a whole new beginning – one that I am excited about."

Annie's story

Age at marriage: 28
Age at break-up: 37

Any children?
Two daughters aged 13 and 12, one son aged almost five

What was the cause of the split?
My husband had an affair with his boss (female) who owned the

organisation he worked for. He was my second husband and the father of my son. My two daughters who lived with us were from my first marriage. He too had been married before.

What efforts did you make individually or as a couple to save the marriage?

I tried, he didn't. He did agree to come back at one point but his girlfriend bought him a new car …

If you turned to professionals in what ways did they help?

My solicitor was useless. He didn't seem to have a clue what to do and the whole legal process seemed to make things worse. In the end I came to an agreement that I would keep the house (which had been mine anyway when we married, although we later put it in joint names) and forgo maintenance. My husband had left me to be with a very wealthy woman whom I had known (and disliked) before and I did not want to take what would have been her money. This was not very bright of me as I was left with three young children, a mortgage and no income.

How did you sort out the financial and residence issues?

My precarious financial situation meant it was extremely difficult to manage. Eventually I agreed that my husband should look after our son so that I could work. I don't know how it happened (that whole period is grey and foggy) but after a while I must have agreed that our son should live permanently with him, with me having access at weekends. The minute this was made legal they moved away to another part of the country. I tried, through solicitors (worse than useless) to gain access but lost contact with my son from the time he was eight. I wrote to him weekly but never heard back. I learnt afterwards that he'd been sent to boarding school.

My mother-in-law, with whom I'd been good friends, wrote and told me that her son (my ex-husband) had threatened to cut her out of his life if she had any contact with me.

My daughters were fine and we became very close. Much later my son somehow discovered that his sister, my elder daughter, was at university in the west of England. They met and carried on meeting while he went to university in Durham. My daughter kept these meetings secret. My son was worried that his father would not support him through university if he re-established contact with us.

The day of his 21st birthday, through my daughter, he contacted me and came home. It was the most traumatic and joyful day of my life. That was nearly nine years ago and we have become very close. He lives in the north with his girlfriend and their children. He has not been back to his father's house for nine years, although he keeps in touch with him.

How were you affected, emotionally and physically, by the split?

Badly affected emotionally; I felt very alone, lost a lot of weight and went to pieces. Gradually I pulled myself together and made a new circle of friends.

How did you cope when you were living alone?

When I was at my lowest I was a real pain, whingeing for hours on end over the phone to friends. One friend told me sharply it was time I pulled myself together and stopped feeling sorry for myself. That was the best thing that could have happened. We're still good friends.

Would you have done anything differently?

It's hard to say but maybe I would go to a better solicitor who specialised in family matters.

Perhaps I should also have tried to be more realistic. I was stubborn, refusing to be dependent on a man who didn't want me any more and, because of that, lost my son. The thought of being supported in that way was abhorrent but I was letting my emotions rule my head.

How long did it take to put your life back together, or at least to feel like facing the world?

About three years. I went through hell wondering what was happening to my son, although I know now he actually enjoyed boarding school and university and had lots of friends. He had no family life and for this I cannot forgive my husband. I don't think you get over the loss of a child, even if, as in my case, the child comes home in the end. We enjoy each other's company a great deal now and are very alike. I have no feelings at all for my husband, probably because I've buried them. I think they would be beyond contempt and I don't know what my reaction would be were I to see him again.

How has your life evolved since the break-up?

When I had my confidence back, I applied for, and got, a good job. In the early years I also developed new interests, made new friends and made it a rule never to turn down an invitation. The single years were good in that I made lots of new friends, developed new interests and learnt to be flexible and adaptable.

When I was 40 I met the man with whom I now live.

Any advice for others?

- Get a good solicitor.

- Know that the black tunnel is something you will emerge from.

RESIDENCE

The issue of residence (previously known as custody) can be one of the most upsetting and enduringly painful aspects of divorce, not just for the children and their parents but also for the wider family of grandparents, aunts, uncles and cousins.

Hearts get broken as the residence order is fought over and the courts decide on the details of the contact order (access). It can all seem so remote from the day you cuddled up together for a family photograph.

Now, with happy family life no longer on the agenda, your own role as a full-time mother or father is at stake.

Opinion is divided on whether or not the courts always meet their obligation to put the welfare of the child above everything. There have been some spectacularly crass decisions over the years that have left all parties – child, mother and father – despairing. But with so much at issue it is inevitable that not every decision will be warmly received.

That's where support groups and campaigning organisations can be your salvation and your strength [see *help box at end of chapter*].

The general thinking is that if you and your ex can work out an amicable agreement between you regarding the children then that will be better all round, for everyone. It means that the grandparents, who often get overlooked when families break up, still have a chance to remain in touch and play their important role in the children's lives, and the children themselves are less likely to be used, even if unwittingly, as pawns in a legal struggle.

The message from those who've been there before is, quite unequivocally, steer clear of the courts. Because it's an adversarial situation, someone is bound to win – and someone is bound to lose.

The expert says...

A parish priest and father of three, the Rev David Smith, aka 'The Fighting Father', has created a website [www.fatherdave.org] where he lets his experience of custody battles stand as a warning to others. He offers these three very basic rules:

1 *Don't go to court.*
2 *Don't go to court.*
3 *Find out everything you can about your situation – where you stand ethically and legally – and use this knowledge to avoid going to court.*

Richard's story

Age at time of marriage: 22
Age at time of break-up: 32

Any children?

Two daughters, aged five and three

What was the cause of the split?

The official cause was adultery on the part of my wife with an Army captain – at least that is what was cited in High Court, which is where it ended up due to my efforts to gain custody of our children. However, the underlying cause was probably that I inadvertently took my wife for granted – thinking that she was happy being at home, mainly looking after the children, when in fact she was not intellectually stimulated enough during the day while I was at work.

What efforts did you make individually or as a couple to save the marriage?

My wife did not make any effort whatsoever to save the marriage. After all, she was desperately in love with another man.

Having gone through severe mood swings (anguish, anger, jealousy) in the initial period, I went to considerable lengths to save the marriage as I loved her greatly and certainly wished to keep the family united.

I plucked up the courage to visit a marriage guidance counsellor with whom I had several sessions on my own and we finally persuaded my wife to balance it up by having some on her own, as well as joint sessions thereafter. At the time, I thought they did a lot of good, so much so that we booked a holiday in the Algarve for three weeks on our own – plenty of laughter, cuddles, sex and meeting nice acquaintances in and around our villa. However, my efforts were soon dashed as she took up with her lover again immediately we returned home.

Prior to the Algarve trip, I did everything in my power to try to save our marriage. I was much more attentive towards her and interested in her, giving her flowers, inviting friends to dinner, dining out. However, having told me about the affair, she then felt she had licence to do exactly what she wanted and stayed out practically every night at his place for the next six months or so, in fact until we went to court.

This was an exceedingly difficult time for me in that I had to take a lot of time off from work to look after the children with school runs, meals, and so on. Worse still, whenever my wife was at home, I had to endure incessant phone calls from her lover at all hours of the night, usually uttering sweet nothings to each other while I lay next to her. On occasions, he insisted on her handing over the phone to me and he found reasons to rebuke me and swear at me and, worse still, tell me that she'd much prefer to be in bed with him than me! This was most hurtful as I was very much in love with her at the time and indeed for at least a year or so after our divorce.

If you turned to professionals, in what ways did they help?

The middle-aged woman counsellor was very good, better than I might have expected; she probed quite deeply and obviously had a lot of experience. She seemed to know how to lift my spirits and give me hope that something may come out of our tattered marriage. On the other hand, my wife appeared to be under duress; all she wanted was to go off with her lover, leaving me with the kids. The counsellor tried very hard to get us together again. She was most disappointed to learn later that we had not succeeded.

My solicitor was thoroughly useless and I got the impression he was more on her side than mine. Her solicitor wiped the floor with mine on most counts, which is why she eventually won the case in High Court. Added to which she had a good barrister whereas mine hadn't read his notes properly and just wanted to get away so he could go and play squash.

How did you sort out the financial and residence issues?

In order not to hurt the children any more than necessary, my wife and I agreed that I would have access every Sunday to begin with. A few weeks later she suggested whole alternate weekends so as to make herself available at weekends for other interested parties. Her affair lasted about eight months when her lover chucked her for a newer model. Although distraught, my wife vowed never to get married to anyone after our divorce, which by this time was imminent.

As the judge awarded her care and control of the children, which meant that she needed a house with at least three bedrooms, our five-bedroom family home was sold a year after our divorce and she received 80% of the proceeds to buy a new home. As her need was greater than mine, she also took the family car and most of our belongings.

As I lost the High Court case, I had to pay all her and my legal costs. This, and the fact that I had heavy monthly maintenance payments, meant I was rather broke for an awfully long time.

How were you affected, emotionally and physically, by the split?

I was deeply affected. I was on the verge of a breakdown due in part to the prolonged lack of sleep over several months.

I also worried that I'd lose my job because I couldn't concentrate, but my boss told me not to worry about it and take as much time off as I needed, which I did, without consequence.

I felt very much like a leper at the time as I appeared to be frowned upon by most of our friends, as if I was to blame for the split, which was not the case. I also felt ashamed that I was beginning to crack up and I couldn't stop legal proceedings.

I was also very affected by the judge's decision to award my wife custody and care and control, despite having left me and the children for three months and having committed adultery.

How did you cope when you were living alone?

Luckily, at the time of our break-up, I had a good work friend who could see early on what I was going through, took pity on me and very kindly offered me her spare room at a modest rent, as a lodger, on a purely platonic basis for a year. I formed many other platonic friendships, which definitely helped.

How long did it take for you to get over the break-up?

It took me at least two years to get over our divorce and 'move on'. I vowed never to lose everything again, which is probably why I've never remarried. I began to feel like my old self again after about five years.

Would you have done anything differently?

I would not have got married at the age of 22, if at all. I might also have remarried but I've always been mindful of the adage 'get married and the relationship flies out of the window'.

How has your life evolved since the break-up?

The only thing that didn't change for five years was my job, which was always a stable environment, something much needed in such turbulent times. However, I became bored and sought more excitement and money elsewhere which I found by starting my own company. I fell flat on my face in the first two years but eventually managed to make a go of my business.

Had I been married again, I don't think I could have coped with the uncertainty of being self-employed as well as the crazy work schedules. Socially, being single again was terrific and I soon found I was mixing with some lovely people. I took to being single like a duck to water.

My first long-term relationship started two years after my divorce. She was a comedienne and she'd recently come out of an equally horrible divorce herself. She helped a great deal in putting me back on my feet – and making me laugh again. The children absolutely adored her and couldn't wait for fortnightly weekend visits. Sadly, she was stolen three years later by a 70 year old millionaire. There were two other girlfriends after that but, sadly, neither relationship worked out – and then I met my current partner.

Any advice for others?

- Don't fight through the courts as I did. You'll be less hurt and your next relationship will probably be more successful.

EXTRA HELP

- The website www.direct.gov.uk contains a wealth of factual information and advice on many aspects of everyday life, but for direction on issues with residence, for example, follow the link from the home page via people, parents, family issues and finally to the law section.

- Families Need Fathers is a group primarily concerned with the problems of keeping parents and children in contact after family breakdown. A national network of volunteers provides advice and support on children's issues to separated, divorced or unmarried parents. www.fnf.org.uk

- Family Welfare Association provides social work and social care services to people facing social and emotional difficulties, including family and relationship problems. www.fwa.org.uk

- Fathers 4 Justice (F4J) is a civil rights movement campaigning for a child's right to see both parents and grandparents. The group comprises fathers, mothers and grandparents who believe that Britain is needlessly creating a nation of children without parents and parents without children. www.fathers-4-justice.org

- Gingerbread is a support organisation with 200 groups for lone parents and their families in England and Wales. It offers advice on such issues as the Child Support Agency, contact, divorce and lone parenthood. Helpline: 020 7336 8184 www.gingerbread.org.uk

- National Council for the Divorced and Separated is a voluntary group that offers friendship and happiness through social branches. www.ncds.org.uk

- The Aquila Care Trust (TACT) is a network of self-help groups in UK for the support, understanding and guidance of divorced or separated people. www.aquilatrust.org

- As well as www.been-dumped.com there is www.wifesgone.com which is a website specifically aimed at helping separated and divorced men with emotional and practical problems. There are others like it, for both sexes, that can be sourced via search engines.

CHAPTER 4

Would therapy work for you?

I am simply not robust enough and have had need of further therapy in the years following my divorce when things have piled up on me. However, on the whole I am coping better as a result of some of the marvellous help I have had. *Penny*

Therapy comes in all shapes and sizes to fit the needs of those who want it. As a means of getting through something as life-changing as a broken marriage or long-term relationship it can be immensely beneficial and many attribute their recovery to its varied powers.

A choice of therapies – traditional, alternative or both – is undoubtedly available near you, or even via the internet, so if you feel you need a boost as you endeavour to get properly back on your feet, this could well be the best move you could make.

Coaching, which is another choice, is neither therapy nor counselling. It's about establishing where you are now and where you want to be, and working out how to get from A to B, step by step, over a period of time.

Then there's life coaching or the more specific divorce coaching – and neuro-linguistic programming (NLP) and any number of other devices that aim to help you move forward.

For some, intervention through any type of therapy works wonders, for others it's like the proverbial damp squib. Only you can tell, once you've tried, if it was the right thing to do. This chapter's case studies and experts' advice may help you decide if you want to turn to a trained practitioner.

Louise's story

Age at time of marriage: 21
Age at time of break-up: 30

Any children?

A daughter aged three

What was the cause of the split?

Physical separation, due to his being in the Royal Navy, which highlighted emotional separation and created issues of abandonment. My illness and breakdown instigated the split.

What efforts did you make individually or as a couple to save the marriage?

We both made efforts to communicate our distress but we talked different languages.

If you turned to professionals, in what ways did they help?

Therapy helped me to come to terms with the break-up and the issues involved and also to be clearer about the person I was and what I needed/wanted from my life.

How did you sort out the financial and residence issues?

When we eventually agreed to split the arrangements were financially simple but custody and access to my daughter were difficult due to questions regarding my competence as a mother after the breakdown and anorexia.

How were you affected, emotionally and physically, by the split?

I suffered a breakdown. My emotional pain was expressed physically by anorexia. I was taking the pain out on myself while remaining blind to the emotional process.

How did you cope when you were living alone?

Four main things were instrumental in rebuilding my life:

Finding a good therapist.

Retraining towards a fulfilling career (never having been able to have one while married).

Learning to like and respect myself again.

The 12-step programme (followed by Alcoholics' Anonymous) was very helpful in finding a more spiritual path.

Would you have done anything differently?

No. Looking back it has all been part of the path, although I would like to have avoided all the trauma for my daughter.

How long did it take to put your life back together, or at least to feel like facing the world?

About three to five years of therapy, but it probably took almost a decade to rebuild a sense of self that was not full of negative judgements and to find forgiveness for myself and for my ex.

How has your life evolved since the break-up?

I have been in a 'new' relationship for 12 years, avoiding some of the pitfalls from before and gaining strength and insight from my partner, my family and friends.

Any advice for others?

● Find help and good support at an early stage.

- Keep your self-respect if possible.

- Look after your physical health.

- Keep communication with partner open if possible and keep blame minimal.

- Find outlets for expressing your feelings and gaining insight.

- Forgive yourself for 'failing'.

Alice's story

Age at marriage: 21
Age at break-up: first affair 28; split up 36; divorce 41

Any children?
Three, aged 13, 11 and five

What was the cause of the split?
I ended our marriage. We were incompatible. We grew apart over the years possibly as the result of getting married too young, which I needed to do to escape from my over-protective elderly parents. He'd been my first boyfriend but he turned out to be very like my father in lots of ways.

The fact I had one serious and then a few other shorter affairs did not help. There was a difference in our expectations of marriage, maybe, although we came from much the same area, class and background.

What efforts did you make individually or as a couple to save the marriage?
We had a third child, six years after our second. This was not directly discussed as a saving mechanism although I kind of

regarded it as being so. My husband may not have been aware by then of how bad things were getting.

We also opened a wine bar in a (failed) attempt to do something new and big together. This was after both my parents had died within 18 months of each other. They would have disapproved of this use of their money. I think psychologists call this a displacement activity. Both the wine bar and then the marriage collapsed, the wine bar with a great loss of money.

If you turned to professionals, in what ways did they help?

I, and then we together, went to Relate for marriage guidance counselling. The sessions were helpful – the atmosphere was sympathetic and non-judgmental while at the same time pertinent; probing but only gently so. Ultimately, though, we stopped going and we got divorced, so how successful the sessions were is a moot point.

The woman counsellor was extremely friendly. She and I had a brief correspondence by letter further down the line which I suspect was above and beyond the call of duty and was extremely supportive.

At the time that we went it was called the Marriage Guidance Council [it changed its name to Relate in 1988] and there were no fixed fees so you just gave a voluntary donation based on what you could afford.

When my present husband and I went to our local Relate last year we found it not only a much more structured and psychotherapeutic process but it was also much more expensive. That turned out to be a fairly major factor in our decision to stop going.

I suspect the fact we were in Greenwich may have influenced

the cost. I know a Relate counsellor from the north of England who says that her cost basis and that of the area she works for are set against needs and means.

Some time down the line I went on my own to a Jungian therapist to discuss primarily the breakdown in my then marriage and my other relationships. This kind of psychotherapy is much more structured and demanding and the relationship with the therapist much more at arm's length. Clearly it's based on a system and the therapist is 'required' to keep a distance from the client, no doubt for both their sakes.

It is a much longer and more intense process and one which it is difficult to extricate yourself from. But it provoked a whole range of different feelings and brought out a whole range of different thoughts and references – sometimes ones I didn't know were there. I feel it was successful because I went back to the same person over a period of 10-15 years: she remained helpful and I would go and see her again if I had the need.

Separately, my current husband went to a very expensive therapist when he and his then wife were experiencing marital difficulties (during the time we were having our affair, but before they split). He said he hated it – he felt the guy did nothing but probe into his childhood and his parents' behaviour and ultimately he refused to go any more. (But I have heard this is common in men who never wanted to go in the first place.)

How did you sort out the financial and residence issues?

My husband was actually very realistic and recognised what children needed and what a court would award. We sold the house and I got two-thirds with which I bought a flat in London. He moved to Devon.

I took no maintenance, feeling I didn't deserve or need it. He paid £300 a month for the children, which should have been increased in line with inflation but never was and I failed to challenge that.

The children lived with me so they were near their friends and school and saw their father every weekend in Devon. The eldest often didn't go because he already had other regular sporting activities but they all went to Devon every Christmas and my husband took them away for part of the summer holidays. All this suited me quite well with the exception of the Christmas arrangement.

Their father rarely visited us in London but he did stay involved in children's school activities such as plays and parents' evenings, and in their birthday parties.

The children always told me that they recognised the unhappiness, were glad the rows stopped and preferred us separate and happy to together and unhappy. At the time there seemed no obvious negatives.

My youngest child resented the constant travel up and down to Devon, especially when he became older and his sister was at university so he had to do this on his own. I think he felt that he missed out on his teenage years with his friends in London.

How were you affected, emotionally and physically, by the split?

Endless rows are always draining and have negative effects on everyone. I remember going to the doctor and getting pills at one point, which I didn't take. Physically, I can't remember any special ill-effects but the wine bar would have masked or excused the obvious tiredness.

How did you cope when you were living alone?

I loved being on my own and though it was tricky coping with the children at times it was very rewarding, especially as I had weekends to myself. In a sense I had the best of both worlds.

I resented my husband's nit-picking attitude to money but didn't totally blame him as I felt I had come out of this better.

We have kept in touch and always been able to discuss relatively sensibly and amicably the children's needs and problems and as they have got older we have been able to do this more. Within the last year or so we have become really quite good friends and he has invited me and my present husband to his 60th birthday party, 20 years after we split up.

Would you have done anything differently?

Well, having affairs so soon after marriage was not ideal but obviously there was an imperative there which I could not stop.

I wish I'd tried to be a little more selfish about the children's weekend arrangements. It suited me at the time but I don't think it was quite the best thing for everyone, particularly the youngest.

How long did it take for you to put your life back together, or at least to feel like facing the world?

Not long at all, perhaps because I was the instigator. I relished the freedom and although things were hard they were better than before.

My feelings were almost immediately overwhelmingly of relief and freedom because I recognised that I probably should not have married my husband in the first place.

How has your life has evolved since the break-up?

I had a flat on my own which gave me a feeling of independence and freedom in a way I had never had, mainly because of my over-protective parents. I had a strong support network of friends locally – some single, some married. The children gave me succour and the family was very together.

I had a number of activities (singing and church particularly) which gave me pleasure and a focus, and a satisfying job.

As the children got older I got a job at the BBC and my career began to develop. After five years I moved to ITN and then met a man with whom I started a relationship. We've now been married for three years but our relationship has gone through difficult times. Now we are working at ways of restructuring it into a 'together-but-separate' arrangement in which our weekends are our own except once a month when we spend the weekend together.

Any advice for others?

- Be honest, open with yourself, each other and the children – though the extent to which they can be involved will depend on their personalities, ages and maturity.

- Try to recognise your differences and work out a relationship which suits you both. Above all, work at it and don't take things for granted.

- Don't be afraid to admit mistakes and seek help.

COUNSELLING

Counselling aims to put you in your control of your life but it's a system that relies very much on your honesty and on how much information you are prepared to divulge about your circumstances. Half a story told is only ever going to result in half the amount of necessary help being received.

Talking to someone who has no emotional involvement – in other words, a trained counsellor as opposed to a member of the family – can help you offload some of your bitterness and take positive steps towards a satisfactory conclusion.

Relate's trained counsellors see more than 100,000 people a year (they're not all trying to save flaky marriages or aid recovery from the fallout) and 90% of those who are counselled say that as a result they understand their problem better and are more able to deal with it.

The counsellor's role is to listen, to help you open up and talk about your concerns, and to help you decide for yourself about how you want to move forward.

Counselling is a tried and trusted method of aiding recovery. It's always good to have an impartial third party to talk to, especially when it's someone who has been trained to know how to respond constructively.

It isn't a magic formula though. One woman who went along with her husband to what she hoped would be a series of sessions to save their marriage, saw to her horror that this man she was prepared to spend the rest of her life with had taken a very obvious shine to the good-looking female counsellor. If I can't trust him in here of all places, she thought, then I'm never going to be able to trust him. The flirting continued, much to the embarrassment of both her and the counsellor, but the marriage didn't.

Penny's story

Age at time of marriage: 26
Age at time of break-up: 50

Any children?
Son 20, daughter 17

What was the cause of the split?
My husband developed manic depression in his twenties, three years after we were married. After many, many years I could cope no more and divorced him.

What efforts did you make individually or as a couple to save the marriage?
A major amount from the start, despite several separations.

After the illness was finally diagnosed and treatment was begun, the prognosis was given to me and the effect it would have on my husband if I should leave him. I also had a son by then who I felt needed a father. Despite leaving me for another woman my husband came back to me, possibly for the sake of his son, although I never knew the reason. My son was under a year old.

If you turned to professionals, in what ways did they help?
I had been torn in two for years living with a man who I some-times cared for and sometimes hated. As a result I was on anti-depressants. I had had a breakdown some six years after we lived together again. I had decided to have another child, how-ever, after speaking to professionals, as I was concerned that my son would have the burden of coping with his father's problem alone otherwise.

I had therapy for over a year before finally taking the step of beginning divorce proceedings.

My husband's psychiatrist, who also treated me later on, said, when I finally told him of my decision to get divorced, that he was so sorry for my husband and that he had not realised he had personality problems quite apart from the manic depression!

Since divorce I have recognised my total inability to handle this terrible illness. I am simply not robust enough and have had need of further therapy in the years following my divorce when things have piled up on me. However, on the whole I am coping better as a result of some of the marvellous help I have had.

My solicitor is a very special personal friend of mine with whom I am in regular contact. She fought passionately on my behalf and acted well, despite having considerable problems with my husband at the time. She realised I needed advice and protection as we were both dealing with a psyche that was not consistent or rational at times.

How did you sort out the financial and residence issues?

In view of his illness, a full and final settlement was agreed. My children chose not to see their father for some time but now, in their maturity, have opened up communication. I am glad to say that my ex-husband has remarried and his wife is stronger than I am and has remained with him. Were it not for her, there would be many, many more problems for my children.

I think both the children have fully recognised now what living with their father was like for me. They have seen him have further manic sessions when he is particularly unpleasant.

Both are now married and have children of their own. My greatest pleasure is seeing, so far, that they are committed within their marriages, realistic about life and its difficulties and pleasures. I have a good relationship with them both.

How were you affected, emotionally and physically, by the split?

Physically I am OK and I'm told I look younger than my years.

Emotionally I have been unable to form a successful relationship with men subsequently and realise that I lost many years
of learning how to 'grow and mature emotionally', focusing
entirely on my children and my nursery school work with small
children with whom I felt valued and at ease.

How did you cope when you were living alone?
I continued to work with small children for a further 10 years
after my divorce. That was my passion and my therapy. It was
also important because my own children needed me to keep up
a position for them.

Would you have done anything differently?
No.

*How long did it take to put your life back together, or at least to feel
like facing the world?*
It has been a struggle but I think I can truly say I have let it go
now, more than 15 years on. I did realise a year ago when I was
on the end of one of my ex's manic attacks how deep the
wounds are and how they make me ill too. I have told my children, which I'd never done before, about the extent of their
effect on me.

I have managed to shed the bitterness I felt that I was totally
ignorant of the illness being in the family and the fact that it
was never discussed. I was deeply hurt, too, by his father and
mother who did little to support me after my decision to
divorce their only son.

I will always remain fond of the kind man I married, before his
illness took him over.

How has your life evolved since the break-up?

I hate being alone and single. Fortunately, I have good friends. I have many interests and follow them up where I can.

I have tried to meet men but while I can laugh about it now I have been very vulnerable and generally the relationships, however brief, cause me stress. I have had to stop trying so hard!

Any advice for others?

- Be self-reliant. It's more peaceful.
- Stay true to yourself and examine your actions and emotions.

The expert says…

"Relationships fire our emotional buttons," says Ariana Gee, who was a Relate counsellor before becoming a relationship coach. "It's our buttons of childhood that are being pressed so that something that happens, or somebody you meet, triggers memories of, say, your first day at school – a momentous experience early in your life. It's not what's happening at that moment, but an interpretation of what happened in your past.

"Some people just aren't able to rid themselves of what went before. It is very difficult to move on, to establish a new and positive relationship that makes you happy, unless or until you have cleared away that baggage. Of course you might want to fill the empty spaces in your life, but you run the risk of repeating past mistakes, perhaps getting into a relationship with someone very like the person you were once married to, and it all turns sour."

Rebecca's story

(It has not been possible for me to answer the questionnaire as it is too painful for me. I've just written what I can as a narrative.)

I was 22 when I got married and 27 when the marriage ended. I'm 30 now. We have no children. I moved from London to America to live with my husband so have no family around me.

It took me about a month to make the decision to leave my husband. During that period I was severely depressed, emotionally unstable and felt desperate. The day I finally decided to leave him was incredibly sobering and I felt a very deep sadness, but these feelings were infused with anger which made it easy to take the plunge and walk out the door.

As soon as I left, I was overwhelmed by a feeling of euphoria. It was as if the doors to my life had opened again and I was free.

However, over the next few years, I learned that getting over a relationship was an emotional roller coaster. Every day brought a different emotion. Some days I felt strong and happy, others deeply depressed.

There would be weekends that I wouldn't get out of bed. Depression was really hard to deal with, but I learned that it was like suffering from 'flu. I understood it was something you had to ride out, and in time it went away.

When our marriage broke up I turned to individual therapy almost immediately. Seeing a therapist one-on-one gave me an opportunity to speak with someone who was completely neutral and could provide a professional as well as an unbiased opinion.

I made the decision to live alone because I had a string of room-mates who wanted to dictate how I should live my life and deal with the end of my marriage. I realised I needed to live alone in order to make clear decisions and to establish a feeling of individuality and independence again. At first it was extremely hard. It took me about a year to feel comfortable with living alone. During my marriage I had lost my sense of self, which living alone helped me regain.

It's taken me just under three years to get my life properly back on track. I never allowed myself to bury any emotions. I've worked very hard to maintain a relationship with my ex-husband and reach a place of peace and friendship with him.

I don't think it's productive to build resentments and hostilities towards someone. It took several years of therapy, and lots of talking and thinking to reach this place.

Ending a relationship is a process. You should never feel forced to get over the relationship faster than you are capable of. It takes time to heal.

HOW THERAPY WORKS

It's all about acquiring the right tools and resources to restore your self-esteem and enable you to cope with change, equipping you for moving onwards and upwards.

"When someone comes to see me I don't know what their story is," says David Plimmer, a holistic practitioner and multi-disciplinary counsellor based in Dorset. "I don't know how resourceful they are, how articulate they might be, what complications they might have encountered that would affect the whole process, whether they are coming from a physical, mental, emotional, spiritual perspective, so I play it by ear. The skill is in getting them to feel comfortable so they will talk freely about why they need my help.

"Some people take the view that having counselling would be an admission that they are taking themselves too seriously. I don't see it that way. Some might feel embarrassed because they think they have brought shame on the family by being divorced, and that can complicate their feelings.

"When someone's marriage has ended I treat them as though they have suffered a loss. I spell out the grieving process which helps explain why they're feeling as they are. They can be encouraged to know that what they are feeling is just a part of the process.

"If someone feels as though they're having a nervous breakdown then it's more than likely they are just grieving. They get so fed up with being miserable. They say to me 'I just want to laugh again. I want to be happy' so I help them to find that state they are seeking.

"What therapy and self-development work does is to allow people to access the resources that are dormant within them and use them. Until you find the resources to get through it can be very isolating and stressful.

"Important in the 'moving on' process is acceptance. This means acceptance of the situation where you are alone, no longer part of a partnership. For instance, if the phone goes your first thought is 'Is that him?' or 'That'll be my wife' – followed by the realisation that it obviously wouldn't be. The disappointment shakes you up a bit.

"Seeing other couples out together is pretty difficult. Seeing other people happy can hurt too much, so you end up not going out. But counselling gives you the tools to cope with those situations.

"I can safely say that 90% of people move on. They probably would have done anyway, without counselling, but this way they gain more skills and resources and their situation is resolved more quickly and painlessly.

"Breaking up makes us stronger but it's a tough way of doing it. You need to be pretty robust to survive it."

David, who also occasionally uses alternative therapies such as soul retrieval and re-birthing to help people recovering from relationship breakdown, charges £42 a session. "It lasts about an hour, give or take a bit either way," he says. "The cost can vary though: some people just give me a box of vegetables."

The expert says...

David is a great believer in the use of affirmations – positive thoughts that you repeat over and over so that your mind focuses on good things rather than thinking negatively. The idea is that you become more aware of your strengths and so your confidence increases.

Affirmations work on the sub-conscious, the same as hypnotherapy, so avoid ifs, buts and negatives or it will only hear that word, David advises. Here are ten that he recommends for anyone lacking confidence as a result of a relationship breakdown:

1 *I am a warm, friendly, well-liked person*
2 *I need to let go of what I no longer need*
3 *I no longer react, I only respond (this one helps with anger)*
4 *It is OK to move on*
5 *It is OK to change*
6 *It's OK being who I am*
7 *I trust in myself*
8 *It is OK to think differently*
9 *I forgive and release everyone in my life*
10 *I can be my own person*

Lisa's story

Age at marriage: 36
Age at break-up: 43

Any children?

Two, aged eight and six

What was the cause of the split?

The cause remains a mystery; I just knew that I was living a lie and that I was miserable.

I didn't feel attracted to my husband. He was a good man, a great father, he was always there for me and the children. In fact he was too much there and I felt stifled. I think I didn't know what I wanted and couldn't have the space to find it. I just knew I didn't want what I had and anything would be better.

What efforts did you make individually or as a couple to save the marriage?

We'd been to Relate three years previously and I asked if he would come again the second time round and he refused, saying it was too much 'navel gazing'. I went on my own.

My husband continued life as normal after I said that it was over (we had to live together for a further six months until the work on the house was completed) and it was as if nothing was going to change. He still occasionally came home with flowers or little gifts.

If you turned to professionals, in what ways did they help?

I had just started to work with a life coach who helped me t garner strength and courage and speak the truth. She was a p lar of strength, always supporting what I chose, though

made quite certain I looked at all options before proceeding along a course of action. Eventually she could take me no further (a coach isn't qualified to do therapy work) and I recognised the need for me to get help to remove the negativity. I chose to speak to a psychotherapist with whom I only worked for a few sessions as I was able to see quite quickly what the blocks were and she helped me move through them at speed.

My solicitor happened not to be a family law specialist but he was in tune with me and was the perfect lawyer. His mantra throughout was "Keep the moral high ground". It is so easy to slip into vengeful tactics, or to expand upon certain trivialities, or to contrive a more compelling piece of evidence. But can you look yourself in the mirror days later, months or even years later? I wouldn't or couldn't have, so I played it straight.

How did you sort out the financial and residence issues?

It was intended to be simple, amicable and with minimal expense but it took what seemed an interminable length of time to sort everything and there appeared to be such long periods of stalling and non-activity. I was keen to get it over with and perhaps he wasn't. Just gathering the financial facts dragged on for over a year.

Seven months after our physical separation and a year after telling my husband it was over, I met someone else. He lived 200 miles away. After six months of a long-distance relationship, with me still in Scotland, the only way I felt that I could find out if we had something which would work was to move closer. I chose to rent a house near him and told my husband that I would be moving there two months later with the children.

Two days after explaining this to my husband I was issued with a court order banning me from taking the kids out of the area

until further notice. On the day the ban was issued, he got on a plane and flew abroad with the kids. I didn't know if he would return but in fact he was gone for three weeks.

I attended court and a CAFCASS [Children and Family Court Advisory and Support Service] reporter was also there. This man, a normal family law solicitor appointed by the court and with no specific training, duly visited both homes, both grandparents, various friends and also visited my intended new rented home.

On the day of judgment in court, the presiding sheriff practically threw the document out for its degree of bias. She went so far as to say that if she were to be pushed, and she wouldn't be, the children would be granted to me, the mother.

Then there were interesting turns in events. My ex chose a new solicitor – one particularly well known for being adversarial and also for winning. Luckily I was unaware of this man's reputation until the week before the next big judgment – a week in court – or I might have bottled it. And what a week it was. I was in the dock for longer than the man who was being questioned for murder in the court next door. At the end of the week, I offered not to move if the judge didn't award the children into my primary care.

Coming to a conclusion took the judge more than 10 weeks and at the end of all that she made no judgment and took my offer as the answer. Life was to continue as it had been since separation.

This took no account of the reality of the situation or of any changes which might happen in the future. What was the point of the exercise? It shows that while everything else is in flux, at least the school is a good anchor.

Ultimately, in order that the children continue at the same school, and because I was left with very little money, I moved back to live with my parents. But as the distance between the two houses and my parents and school was too far, I chose to suggest that they live with him full-time with me having an afternoon per week and every second weekend. This gave them the stability they sorely needed.

Shared care is a fine idea but in practice is not necessarily as good as it first appears. Also, as a mother who had been wholly responsible for the children, I gave away my status of primary carer and lost it for ever. I let that stand as a warning.

How were you affected, emotionally and physically, by the split?

I felt guilty as the perpetrator of a crime – to break up a family for no apparent reason other than being unhappy. Also, so much time is spent on high alert that adrenalin is charging your system. The quoting of facts from 'the other side' provokes anger as they are so often misconstrued or exaggerated.

Physically, I suffered from stress-related symptoms such as panic attacks, hives all over my body, and later I also suffered from terrible heartburn and sickness.

How did you cope when you were living alone?

At first it was strange, but luckily I had a dog which required regular walking, feeding and stroking. I was used to being in charge of household bills and nothing was new to me except things like putting up curtain rails and other DIY jobs.

I enjoyed the space, the quiet and it gave me time to think and grieve. There was a lot of grief, not for the marriage, but for the hatred, the vindictiveness and my guilt.

My family and close friends supported me through the whole thing, without any word of caution about what I was taking on as they could see how miserable I was in the marriage.

Is there anything that you would you have done differently?

Yes, I do wish I had not been governed by fear. Many of my actions were, in retrospect, fear-related. I found it difficult to speak my truth as I knew I'd be silenced.

I would love to have been able to discuss openly and honestly what I was hoping for from my future, and listened to his views. He threatened me 15 months before I said I was moving when he told me, "Don't you even think of trying to take the children away or I'll fight you every inch of the way." I knew I was damned whatever I did and would only ever be able to live by his rule book.

How long did it take to put your life back together, or at least to feel like facing the world?

To begin with it felt I had it back together within days of moving out. Then when court started life went on hold again for the full nine months. After that was all over, I found a ledge and started to live again, only to find there was no fire in my belly driving me forward. Everything caved in and I was worse than I'd ever been for a few months – that was more than two years post-separation. I reckon it took me three years and a great deal of help to regain control of myself and my life.

I've worked hard at allowing the feelings to come through and not bury them. Burying them means denying them and they'll always come up and bite your bum again. I've learnt not to ask for any changes unless I'm prepared to go back to court. I won't get them, nothing will change.

How has your life evolved since the break-up?

My own self-development work and training have allowed me to grow and learn in ways I would never have imagined. I have found what I was looking for – to be responsible for my own happiness and to love myself – only then is it possible to enter a fulfilling relationship with someone else.

I needed to be able to release the negative emotions. I did this by training as an NLP [neuro-linguistic programming] practitioner. I've also continued training in ways to make anger, fear, sadness and guilt disappear quickly and easily. I know for a fact that without physically removing them I would not be able to express all this or be able to realise a fantastic life for myself, let alone give hope to others.

Any advice for others?

- There is no point in sweeping emotion under the carpet – it is a traumatic and difficult life-change. It is an opportunity to go beyond yourself and re-brand into something bigger and better. They say religion is where you turn when you want to save yourself from hell; spirituality is where you turn when you've been there.

- Always remember, your children will love you no matter what – you really don't need to see them daily for that to be the case. It's a tough call, but it's true. You need them more for your sake than for theirs.

HOW NLP WORKS

Jackie Walker has a Master Practitioner qualification in neuro-linguistic programming (NLP) and uses the technique in her work as a divorce coach, employing a combination of counselling, therapy and coaching alongside occasional spiritual healing.

She says of her work: "I provide the sixth emergency service to those who are in the midst of total collapse of their universe but who still know somewhere deep inside that 'all will be fine'. They are just struggling to know what to say, do and be. I'll hold their hand and keep them afloat until they're ready – and then the fun begins."

Jackie's approach depends on what stage the client is at in the divorce procedure and, as she explains, whether they are "the dumper or the dumpee – the one who has been dumped".

"There's quite a bit of catch-up to be done if you're the dumpee," she says, "but to be honest a lot of the dumper's work is done prior to the break-up. However, they are more likely to suffer from guilt, which they need to get rid of pretty rapidly. The dumpee can tend to carry the 'victim or martyr' role for years without help.

"If someone comes to me in the depths of despair, I spend a long time holding their hands (metaphorically) and getting the story, the background, their personal history basically, which often shows up as the same 'stuff' as they faced all along and probably stems from childhood. This is true whether it's the dumper or the dumpee.

"The dumper probably finds that their partner isn't stacking up to expectations any more, or that they made a wrong choice to get something which had eluded them for years, or that the fear they had years ago now seems to have vanished. Unfortunately, what tends to happen is that once out of what seemed to be a prison, the old fear re-materialises and they then start to re-enact their old patterns. This is when it's fundamental for them to get help – to become aware of the patterns in the first place, to find out what the fears are, and then get rid of them. This usually turns out to be something along the lines of the fear of not being good enough/not being significant to someone else/not being liked/living alone/looking stupid and Billy no-mates.

"The dumpee, on the other hand, has all the same fears, but they weren't in control of when it happened. It stands to reason then that they feel justified in adopting the mantle. Most dumpees find it difficult to accept that they had any part to play in the circumstances which led up to the divorce/separation.

"I believe that there is no smoke without fire and both parties are responsible.

"The ability to stand on one's own two feet is paramount in separation/divorce scenarios. It is the move from co-dependent to independent which enables the person to have self-confidence, self-esteem, courage and the ability to love first themselves and secondly anyone else."

The expert says...

Jackie believes there are various reasons for the remarkable increase in calls for divorce coaching and therapy:

- People expect to have help available.

- Families and close friends tend to be more far-flung nowadays.

- The relationship breakdown has increased enormously.

- Self development is much more accepted and expected these days.

- *Divorce needs to be seen through new eyes. The increase in divorce rates is not new, it just keeps growing, therefore it is normal (like it or not). Every other life-change has some support service and divorce has been very much on the back burner until now.*

- *Legal fees can be reduced if you take the time to look after yourself before lambasting your ex — you learn communication, perspective and what is driving you in your anger, fear, sadness and guilt.*

- *Lawyers aren't trained in giving emotional advice.*

- *There are a lot more self aware people out there who are prepared to make the changes to themselves which are necessary in order to help them move forward and enjoy a fulfilling, loving relationship.*

Treating a client

(Jackie Walker recounts how she helped Jane, aged 43.)

Jane contacted me 10 months after her marriage had broken down as she'd had an affair. She moved out of the family home and for 10 months had been negotiating with her husband via the legal teams for a financial settlement. Her relationship with the other man wasn't progressing well (he was married too). Jane was extremely attractive, well groomed and her three children aged 21, 18 and 15 continued to see both her and her husband.

Jane was finding it very difficult to know what to do – should she go back to her husband and the family home or should she persevere with the new man? With my input she uncovered the real reasons why she got married, why she stayed in the relationship for so long, and why she now felt the way she did.

She had an enormous fear of being on her own, of looking stupid on the social scene without a man and of not being good enough. She hadn't worked in over 20 years. How would she support her lifestyle, she didn't know who she was other than a wife or mother, she was afraid of being herself because … who was she?

It took a few hours of working with her to get all the fears, the sadness, anger and guilt out into the open – things which she'd bottled up and put away on the top shelf. At the same time it's important to find out what the client wants these things replaced with – how do they really want to feel?

We then started on the therapy work, removing all the negative emotions using timeline therapy, which allows you to release the pain using a very safe, effective and speedy methodology. I then give a Huna energy session to balance the energies in the body (it's optional, but so relaxing and works fantastically at this stage).

Thereafter, the stage is set for building up a new life. We identify what the client wants to create, what steps are necessary to get there, we build the picture and then work backwards to find the starting point.

Life takes some form of deliberation – some intention is required if you want to feel fulfilled. How do you know you're miserable or happy unless you know what you want your life to look like?

So, back to Jane. She'd never planned more than a holiday in her life, so we used the holiday to plan her future. She wasn't going on a fast jet yet, more of the slow canal boat. But she found where she wanted to go. She wanted to be important in someone's life, she learned how to be important to herself first so that she would always recognise when things were going well, or not.

She found that she had creative ideas of what she could do to bring in some money and she set about dreaming her big dream and who would be able to help her make it come true. Then she addressed the communication issue with her ex. By this time she was able to accept that she was responsible for the way he spoke back to her because the meaning of communication is in the response we get. She learned to phrase things differently, to be open and honest in her communication with him, she learned to put herself in his shoes and see what the effect might be. She found that making decisions alone suddenly seemed to be fun, that she was in control of what she said and did and had no one else to blame.

The other man? He's history – she found that she didn't need a man to be significant. She wanted a man – but only the man who would have an equal, loving relationship would be good enough. In the meantime, the nights at home alone gave her time to remind herself how important she was, for the chance to build a dream life for herself now, how grateful she had become to her ex-husband for the life they had had, what she had learned, and for their three children.

GEMMA'S SNAPSHOT

Carl and I weren't married but we'd been going out together for nine years, since my last year at school. Our little boy was born just after we moved in together four years ago. We were really happy at first. Carl went away a lot because he drives lorries so I brought the baby up on my own, pretty much.

One night we left the baby with a friend and went to the pub for the evening. On the way home Carl pushed me into the corner of a car park and raped me. It was the worst thing that has ever happened to me in my life. It changed everything.

I was only 25 but I felt my life was over. I couldn't bear to look at Carl again, or even be in the same room as him. He took his things and left. Good riddance.

My doctor arranged for me to have therapy. I had seven sessions with a really nice woman and it helped a lot. I still have nightmares but not as bad as before. At first it was tempting to go back and live with my dad, because he offered. He was being kind, but I thought if I did that I'd probably never get out and anyway the baby would drive him mad.

Now I'm getting on OK and I've heard that Carl is having treatment to get him off drugs. I had no idea he was on drugs. It makes me very sad.

I got on to the Child Support Agency to make Carl support Reece. I've had a few payments, nothing much, and I don't suppose I'll get anything more.

Looking after the baby isn't easy but it gives me something to get up for every day. Knowing he's my responsibility has made me concentrate on getting better. I'm hoping to get a job one day which will fit in with his pre-school and then his school, later on.

Ann's story

Age at marriage: 23
Age at break-up: 48

Any children?
Three, aged 19, 17 and 13

What was the cause of the split?
I presumed, as so many people do, that I was still happily married after 24 years. It was my birthday, I was away from home and was about to address a big NHS conference in my capacity

as a consultant. I found myself having lunch with a senior person in the NHS who knew my husband quite well as they'd worked together.

Over lunch, in a way that wasn't intended to destabilise me at all, he said: "Your husband's a bit of a one for the ladies – and the men too, I hear." So that was my introduction to the fact that all was not well.

He then went on to tell me that Mark was having affairs with a couple of the nurses at the hospital where he worked and was also having a gay affair with a fellow consultant.

So instead of doing my speech from the platform I went and sat in my car in the car park for several hours while I absorbed all this and rewrote history, as you do.

I went home and gradually it all emerged. I would never have dreamt of looking before, but the evidence was all around me: his car was full of condoms, there were messages from the gay bloke on his phone and there were photographs on the computer.

How stupid could I be for not knowing? I really didn't have any idea at all. We staggered on for a while but the affairs continued. Eventually, about a week after our 25th wedding anniversary, he left. He gave no clues about what he was going to do. I had no idea even where he was going to live. He took a few shirts and trousers and that was about it.

What efforts did you make individually or as a couple to save the marriage?

For a long time before he left I had tried to invest in doing the reconciliation bit. I have to say that he had had a fantastic relationship with the children up to then and the potential loss was going to be enormous. So if only for that reason I had a vested interest in trying to keep it going.

What really brought it to a head was the humiliation I felt. Twice in the year before he moved out, he brought a partner home. I don't know if they were male or female but he entertained them in my room, in my bed, while I was at work. Twice I dragged the bed down to the end of the garden and chopped it up with an axe and set fire to it. If he had just left, then OK, but that sort of disrespect is just extraordinary.

Three months after Mark left I took the children away on holiday. We had no idea where he was. We returned home and his car was outside the house. The children were overjoyed and cried "Dad's come home!" My heart was in my boots. As we got to the door he just walked past us and said "Oh, terribly sorry – I didn't think you'd be back yet." He went up the garden path and left. That was it. Yet again he had had somebody else in my bed. So that was a third bed that went. After that I changed all the locks.

It came out in court that he had put me at risk of HIV through his behaviour. I was very shocked by that.

I felt really that I was taking part in some very long episode of *Neighbours* and that one of these days I would wake up and be allowed off the screen set.

If you turned to professionals, in what ways did they help?

What happened to me was so ghastly and violent and a whole load of other things that I felt I needed something to keep me on my feet and operating. I had counselling to help me get over the trauma caused by his violence. I had to promise never to be on my own with Mark because I would be putting myself in danger.

Both my daughters had counselling, too, at different times in the aftermath.

About two years ago someone told me about Divorce Recovery Workshops, which sounded interesting. It took a lot of organising to get myself free for a weekend but I enrolled on an intensive, long weekend course in North Devon.

It was run in a way that offered you personal challenges and the opportunity to set yourself goals. It was very, very positive and it really made a huge difference to how I thought about myself.

Since the DRW course I feel I'm much more empathetic than I used to be. The whole experience – the marriage break-up and the experience of the course – has, I think, made me a better person. I certainly feel that the children and I have ended the right way up.

How did you sort out the financial and residence issues?

After I had started divorce proceedings, because it was quite obvious we weren't going to be able to continue like that, he emerged from the woodwork long enough to take me to court. Eventually it all got sorted out as these things do but he fought very, very hard to get me and the children out of the house.

The most difficult thing for me to cope with has been that Mark has divorced the children as well as me. It wasn't a normal divorce. He actually wished to ditch the whole lot of us.

I couldn't allow him to throw us out of the house. The children had had enough problems coming to terms with his leaving but to be thrown out of the house as well would have been too awful.

I had to do absolutely everything. Mark had done nothing at all about sorting out our financial affairs, closing joint accounts or preparing for court. He just insisted that he would not negotiate at all, not on child care, not anything. He put it all in the hands of particularly vicious solicitors and I was left to sort it all. So there were a lot of tears shed in the bank and in various solicitors' offices. The staff at my HSBC branch still get out the box of tissues when they see me come in the door.

I was profoundly shocked at how much worse the court process made the whole thing. It was bad enough anyway but there was nothing about the court process that helped or moved us on in any way at all. It was the adversarial nature of it that I found so shocking.

How were you affected, emotionally and physically, by the split?

The fallout was immense. There was so much going on. I had to get an injunction against the husband of one of Mark's girl-friends who became really quite ill and upset by what was going on. The husband used to come and scream abuse at me from under my bedroom window for failing to keep Mark at home. I am not the sort of person to whom this sort of thing happens and nothing in my life had prepared me. He was also making disgusting telephone calls to me. The injunction was to stop him getting on our property and we had phone calls monitored.

Then the son of one of Mark's girlfriends came round one night and slashed all the tyres on his car. I think it happened twice although Mark never actually admitted why he had had to change the car tyres for a second time – on his 'mid-life crisis' sports car. I actually felt quite unsafe from time to time.

Before Mark moved away he would go out (and I never knew if it was with a girlfriend or a boyfriend) and come back at about 11 o'clock and get into bed with me, at which point I would get up and leave the house. I just couldn't bear to stay there with him. I didn't know where to go or what to do, so I'd drive off and go and stand on the beach for a few hours.

About a year after I found out and as it became clear that it was not going to be resolvable, I got to the stage where I felt I needed someone to talk to. I would be driving back from work and realise that I wasn't in a fit enough state to go into the melting pot that was our home.

I picked out a person – a friend of a friend – who I thought would be able to cope OK and who I felt I would be able to chat to and who knew me well enough before all this, because some of what happened sounded so crazy. I really did – and still do – need someone whose kitchen table I could collapse on now and then. I certainly didn't want someone to pass judgement on Mark at that point.

How did you cope when you were living alone?

In the middle of the mayhem following his departure, my eldest daughter decided to get married. I'd been pretty much OK up to then but suddenly I found I was having days when I would be wedding-dress shopping with my daughter in the morning and filling in six pages of evidence of adultery in the afternoon.

The cognitive difference got too much and I really got very distressed. Even the day before the wedding, when we were doing last-minute alterations to bridesmaids' dresses, putting the finishing touches to the cake and making buttonholes, we had the court bailiffs in the house, sent by Mark, to do a valuation.

I have managed to get on top of the finances and keep the house together, which pleases me. Some of the practical issues have been challenging, to say the least, but fortunately I discovered ladies' nights at B&Q and signed up. There were about 20 of us, all with our orange pinnies, nearly all in the same position as me, saying "How the hell do you change the washer on a tap?" We'd turn up on a Thursday evening at B&Q and get on with our tasks. One night they let us use almost every power tool in the place. Another night we did plumbing and learnt how to do tap washers. It certainly improved my practical skills.

Is there anything that you would you have done differently?

I would like, somehow, to have been able to continue the children's relationship with Mark's parents. I don't know how I'd have done this, because his whole family has had no contact with me since Mark and I separated, not even his brothers and sisters, but I do feel sad that my son, for instance, no longer has that special bond with his grandfather.

How long did it take to put your life back together, or at least to feel like facing the world?

I gave myself five years because I reckoned it was not something I was going to get over quickly. I've got through four so far so I still don't have to beat myself up. As long as I don't have too high expectations, I'm OK. Finding the right friends and other people to talk to and rely on has been a great help to me.

Unfortunately, in a supreme act of aggression and hostility towards me, Mark has chosen to move back to within half a mile of our house. He had been gone for two years and we had just about got used to not having him around and not knowing where he was. He told my eldest daughter but nobody else. My son has found it very, very hard to have his dad living so close but still not to feel welcome.

If we're shopping in the supermarket he may emerge from behind the shelves, somebody in hand, no doubt – and it could be a male or a female. This could be difficult because the children still don't know that their father has gay partners.

As far as my life is concerned, it's quite nice being single again with all the choices available to me. It's actually quite exciting. For instance, I suddenly find I can champion single parents with some degree of experience.

But it's a different relationship you have with your kids, particularly as they move on to sexual relationships of their own, if they know you've fouled up in some way, because you really cannot take the moral high ground. We have a very honest and open relationship with each other, which is fine.

How has your life evolved since the break-up?

Because of the ages of the children at the time our marriage broke up, I've had a lot of work to do single-handed to get them through the various stages of education – GCSEs, A-levels and university.

My son struggled a very great deal with school and life in general and I have had to help him through some really tough times. It was his last day at school that really was my lowest point. It was speech day and he won a prize and all the right things were happening for him to boost his confidence. I would have liked Mark to have been there, not as my husband – we're well past that – but I feel that it would have been the right acknowledgement of his parenting duties.

But of course he wasn't there and I thought: "How could you not even contact me and say well done for what you've achieved with the children?" I had thought I was going to be all upset and weepy about this event marking the end of school days but actually I came away absolutely furious. I had never felt so angry. I felt I had taken some backward steps in my recovery.

I was very surprised by the strength of my anger. I have read about other people feeling like this, wanting to know 'How could you? How dare you?' It turned out Mark was in France with another floozy.

Any advice for others?

- Try to avoid the things that can make you feel very fed up and sorry for yourself, like doing the supermarket shop at 2am.

- When it's all really, really ghastly at the beginning, learn to tackle only that day's problems. Next week's or next month's issues can wait. A very wise friend advised me not to get anxious about what might happen next week – just cope with today.

DIVORCE RECOVERY WORKSHOPS

Feeling stupid, as Ann did, for not knowing your partner is being unfaithful is a natural reaction. In fact it's as natural as the anger that also comes with the shattering discovery. No one likes to find out they've been cheated on, with the possibility that others, friends included, knew all about it and they didn't.

To come across others going through the same turmoil of emotions and facing the same changed landscape is reassuring as well as mutually beneficial. That's one of the many spin-offs of Divorce Recovery Workshops [see *box at end of chapter*], a nationwide network that organises courses to help put emotionally traumatised divorcees back on track and in charge of their lives.

The organisation welcomes anyone at any age and at any stage of their divorce, whether they are the dumper or the one who's been dumped. Support is also given to people from civil partnerships so it's for anyone who has experienced irreversible relationship breakdown.

Recovery workshops are held at various locations around the country and are run by experienced people who have been through the workshop as participants. There are workshops that are held for two hours one evening a week for six weeks or workshops that are held over a long weekend.

According to DRW, these are the most common benefits to be had:

- Enabling individuals to retake control of their present and future.

- Functioning effectively again as a single person, parent or breadwinner.

- Helping restore self-esteem at a time when it's at its lowest.

- Alleviating the tendency towards depression, isolation and suicide.

- Relieving tensions between partners to the benefit of children.

- Speeding up an individual's recovery period.

- Enhancing personal development and growth.

Ruth, who now runs workshops in her home town after attending a weekend course in North Devon, recalls the life-changing experience.

"With all six sessions in three days it was quite intensive, but it was very, very positive and it really made a huge difference to how I thought about myself.

"It was great to meet a whole community of people at every stage, from still very raw, as I was, right through to ten years on and clearly on the other side and doing OK. That was really encouraging.

"The workshop was run in a way that offered you personal challenges and the opportunity to set yourself goals. One of the central tenets of the course is that you learn to take responsibility for your own part in the fact your marriage has failed.

"Then you learn the importance of accepting that it's your marriage that's failed and not you – that's really critical. You can still be a good parent, a good friend, a good employee, all these other roles that you have in life, and a useful member of the community, despite what's happened, so this knowledge helps the divorce to stop spreading and colouring every single aspect of your life.

"There was somebody else from my town who did the same DRW course as me. When we got home we agreed we ought to see if anyone would like to do a course – and of course the minute you say that, lots of people come out of the woodwork. There have been between seven and ten on each course."

Key issues covered in each weekly session are:

1 Is this really happening to me? Accepting and letting go of the past.

2 Assuming new responsibilities – planning for yourself and your future.

3 Coping with your ex-spouse – a relationship reality that continues to exist.

4 Family matters.

5 Forgiving and letting go.

6 Thinking about new relationships.

"Pretty much all of them have to go through some sort of difficult court case," Ruth says, "and only very few of the ones who come to us have been able to reach an amicable agreement. I think that's partly because the court case is so traumatic, especially for parents. For children, the fact that their parents are in court fighting is just the pits.

"DRW sessions touch on practical matters, too. For men it's things like keeping an address book, remembering birthdays and so on; for women it's topping up the car's screen cleaner or oil or – yes, truly – opening the bonnet. We talk about keeping body and soul together, of course, and the importance of living and eating healthily. I try to suggest to the slightly more adventurous men that Jamie Oliver might be a bit less restricting than Delia Smith when it comes to recreating recipes in the kitchen."

EXTRA HELP

- Relate offers counselling for men and women before and after separation, as well as children of divorced or separating couples, for the couples in their role as parents, and for co-parents coping with living apart. 0845 456 1310
  www.relate.org.uk

- Find a therapist near you through the British Association for Counselling and Psychotherapy 0870 443 5219
  www.bacp.co.uk.

- Divorce Recovery Workshops: 07000 781889 www.drw.org.uk to find a contact near you.

- David Plimmer: 01963 363359 www.davidplimmer.co.uk

- NLP and other divorce therapies as well as divorce coaching: Jackie Walker 0800 019 6862 www.thedivorcecoach.co.uk

CHAPTER 5

Getting on with life

The thing I noticed the most post-marriage was the amount of money I saved and so quickly. I have been able to put thousands behind me now and buy myself so much. I have also travelled extensively worldwide. *John*

There is something – no, let's face it, everything – very appealing about turning your back on that whole grisly business of divorce and starting afresh. That can only be a pipedream for most, for whom the life-defining considerations of jobs, houses, schools, mortgages and financial constraints dictate how the aftermath of divorce is going to be lived.

But for those who can and do make a break from the unhappy past, whether it's by moving to another country or taking the plunge into a new career (or both), the future is immediately fresh, different and exciting.

They would be regarded by many as the more fortunate ones, perhaps, although their route to a new way of life may be long and painful. It isn't easy making big-life-changing decisions on your own, especially when you've been used to making even the smallest decisions as part of a twosome. To be weighing up the pros and cons of a house move or a change of job as a new singleton is very different from the days when you would have said "Let's decide together what we're going to do."

That's where family and friends can play their part. They may have helped sustain you through the break-up but their job isn't over yet. There's the next phase to be considered.

Andrea, who tells her story further on, perfectly illustrates the theme of this chapter when she writes of her recovery: "I moved countries, found work and relied on a great network of supportive friends." It's hard to think of any better way of putting the past behind you and starting afresh.

Many of the case studies in this chapter also make it clear how large a part friends and family have played in their lives.

John, suddenly single again and launching a new career, attributes much of his successful recovery to two things: he followed the advice of a friend whose marriage had broken down earlier and absorbed the wise words of his mum.

Felicity, dumped at 55 in favour of a younger model, says she wouldn't have coped without the fantastic support of her sister, her sons and her friends.

Then there's Lynn, who has never married but has battled through the fallout of three long-term relationships. "I count myself lucky not to have children to drag through any break-up," she says, "although in a way it's harder as I don't have flesh and blood distractions.

"But friends are an absolute necessity. Without them, my dad and my brother (strangely, my mother never realised the effect it all had on me) I would have gone under completely. So take my advice: keep up your friends and family connections – even when you feel that your world is complete with your partner."

Finding support

One of the common threads running throughout this book is the crucial part played by friends and family in people's recoveries. Tributes galore are sprinkled through the pages, from Tony's: 'A great group of loyal and supportive friends, plus my family, got me through,' to Duncan's: 'My mates to me were people that I could go out and have a laugh with and if something happened that I needed to get off my chest, I could do, and then get back on with the night out or whatever.'

There are few more certain ways of finding out who your friends really are, and just how close your family ties are, than when your life is turned upside-down by the ending of a relationship. Who is there for you when you really cannot manage without an understanding ear to hear you, when you're sobbing your heart out at 3am and everything just seems too awful for words?

Try and make sure there's someone you can reliably turn to when the need is overwhelming. Don't wait until you're desperate and resort to someone unsuitable or unwilling.

But be warned, the role of family and friend(s) as cheerleader, supporter, No.1 confidant and part-time therapist is all very well, but it may not be as constructive or helpful to your recovery as you might hope.

The expert says . . .

Two divorce coaches, Kirsten Gronning and Jackie Walker, urge caution. "Many people, whether they're friends or family, just don't want to get involved anyway," Kirsten says. "Equally, those in need of support may not feel they want to burden their friends and family. They want to be sure of keeping their friends after the event.

> "For men especially, when they lose their wife they lose a confidante. Women tend to have more friends they confide in, but often friends tell you want they think you want to hear, or what suits them."
>
> Jackie adds: "Family and friends aren't the best when it comes to learning about yourself as they have their own agenda, unwittingly, about what you should do, who you must be, that change isn't necessary, that they'll help get the b*****d who did this to you, and so on. They're quite often happy to fuel your cause, rather than stand back from it."

So take on board these gentle words of caution: friends and family can be great, they can always be there for you, they can make a huge difference to the speed and nature of your recovery, but they may not always know better and they may not always be in the best position to offer you the sort of objective help and support you most need.

Indulge in a little research and planning, like Ann did (*previous chapter*) before she opted to recruit the friend of a friend as her reliable, resourceful, listening mate. She explains: "The last thing I wanted was someone to say what a bastard he was. Only I was able to do that. I'm a doctor so in true doctor fashion I wanted to make sure none of this would be a real problem for this kind woman I'd chosen to be my 'sympathetic ear'.

"I needed somebody to be there when I came back from court or back from visiting solicitors or the bank. The sorts of conversations I needed to have were: 'What do I do about my wedding ring? When do I take it off? Where shall I put it? And please cut up my Barclaycard for me because he's just taken his friend to Barcelona on my credit card. I really can't take this any longer – please, just take the card and do the necessary.'

"This lovely woman went through all of those things with me and she was just the most fantastic support.

"The sort of friends I really valued too, and still do, are the ones who allow us to still have a normal family experience. The really good things were being invited to join another family for Sunday lunch where we were considered normal – it was just that Dad happened not to be there. It feels like a big hole when they're not there at first."

Emma (*this chapter*) says that she enjoys the benefits of a two-dimensional friend – an email penfriend. "She understands me, she knows me, but we just have one-sided conversations as we don't meet and we don't speak. It works wonders!" Whenever she's been at her lowest, Emma says she has found it really useful to write things down, and emailing her thoughts and feelings to her sympathetic friend has been cathartic and helped enormously.

Stephen, ploughing through the early months after his marriage breakdown, says he believes that recovering from a split is something you have to do alone. "Knowing that support is there for when things gets too tough is essential, but in practical and emotional terms, the quicker you can stand alone, the better it is for your own sake.

"That doesn't mean you have to rush into rash decisions, just that if you rely on someone else's emotional strength to get you through – whether that's a new partner, a parent or a friend – be aware you're not actually growing as a person. And somewhere down the line that's going to trip you up once more."

Felicity's story

Age at marriage: 31
Age at break-up: 55

Any children?

Two sons, aged 18 and 20

What was the cause of the split?

My husband left me to pursue an affair with a woman 16 years his junior who worked for him.

What efforts did you make individually or as a couple to save the marriage?

I tried everything I could think of to persuade him to give her up and stay with me. He would have happily stayed with me and carried on the affair but, as far as I was concerned, that was not an option. He eventually decided he would stay and he told her it was over, but two days later I found him on the phone to her. He stayed for three more weeks. The real crunch came when he had to go to the distant branch office (where she worked) and stay overnight and I said I would go with him. It was at this point that he really did leave so I'm quite sure that he had intended to carry on with the affair while living with me.

If you turned to professionals, in what ways did they help?

After he'd gone, we went on one introductory visit to Relate but that was rather a disaster. The person we saw was certainly not right for us and I don't think my husband was very honest. He couldn't wait to get away afterwards to go and meet his mistress.

How did you sort out the finances?

Four years on we are still not actually divorced but we're hoping to do it with as little involvement with solicitors as possible because of the high costs involved. Just over 18 months ago I said I wanted to sort things out and get divorced but he keeps delaying and not doing the things he's promised to do. I've been trying to play it gently in the hope that he will be a little kind to me (probably crazy of me to expect that but I've always been an optimist). I realise the real impetus is going to have to come from me or it will never happen.

How were you affected, emotionally and physically, by the split?

I was hugely hurt by the rejection, very frightened about the future, angry with the way he'd behaved and desperately sad for our two sons and the break-up of the family. There was also disbelief that my husband of 24 years, best friend and father of our sons, could behave like this and abandon us.

I lost about a stone-and-a-half in weight, which was a silver lining to the cloud but a very tough way to do it. I also found it extremely difficult to sleep. For the first year, I rarely managed to sleep for more than two or three hours a night and I think I existed on adrenalin. That has gradually improved but I still frequently have very bad nights. However, I must count my blessings: I wasn't ill and, so far at least, I have survived.

How did you cope with living on your own?

My sister, my sons and my friends have been fantastically supportive and without their help I'm not sure that I would have coped. I play a lot of tennis and kept that up throughout, which has been a real saviour, although I wonder how I didn't collapse in a heap at the net at times.

My two dogs have helped keep a structure to my otherwise solo days.

Since my husband left, I've worked really hard to forge a new career for myself as the work I had been doing as a technical author came to an end a few months before he left. I'm now working between nine and 12 hours a day which, since I am self-employed, is vital if I am to maintain two important contracts.

Although I'm too busy to ever really feel lonely, I do hugely miss the company of another person, the hugs, the evenings spent in the company of someone you love and can simply chill out with. It's been a very big jump from three men in the house to none now that the boys have moved on to university and work. I hate eating meals on my own and have, I'm afraid, resorted to eating my evening meal in front of the television, which used to be taboo.

I don't much like going out on my own, although I make sure I accept invitations as much as possible because I think it's very important to keep my social life going. Although I manage to cope with most things myself, I do get frustrated when a job needs doing in the house which I don't feel able or competent to do. I'm afraid I don't really do drilling.

Would you have done anything differently?
I'm afraid I just do not know.

How long did it take to put your life back together, or at least to feel like facing the world?
I'm not sure I have fully put my life back together – I don't think that's possible until we're divorced. I faced the world pretty quickly in many ways – accepted invitations and so on, but the real turning point was when I made the decision to go to Sweden (*see over*).

Getting over the hurt and learning to trust again is still very hard. My husband wasn't an easy person to live with in many ways, not least because he has a very short temper, but there were plenty of good things in the marriage and I did trust him. Above all I have suffered a huge hurt, a betrayal, a major knock to my confidence and – something I'm very ashamed of – I rather hope he's going to be a miserable old sod in his old age and regret what he did!

I would like to feel more kindly towards him and perhaps one day I will, but right now that's really hard. My friends all said my husband was a fool to go and, as the other woman is still living with her husband three-and-a-half years later, perhaps they were right.

How has your life evolved since the break-up?

I've been extremely lucky to have got back in touch with a Swedish man with whom I was in love 30 years ago before I met my husband. I sent him a card saying that my husband and I were living apart. I didn't know what was going to happen but thought it was a good time to get in touch. I really didn't think I'd ever hear from him but he rang as soon as he got the card. If I hadn't written it, things would be very different.

He invited me to go to Sweden and we found we were still (or again?) in love. It's far from plain sailing and, unfortunately, he has no money so it doesn't help the financial situation. However, the nature of my work means that I can stay with him in Sweden and work there for two to three weeks at a time and he comes to England when he can.

It is simply wonderful to have the love of a kind and caring man and I'm certain that has stopped me from becoming bitter and twisted.

Any advice for others?

Hard, so very hard as it is:

- Believe in yourself.

- Maintain your self-respect.

- Keep going.

- Try not to feel bitter because it harms you more than anyone else.

- To coin a much-used but very helpful phrase, take one day at a time. Each day you get through is a day nearer to recovery.

- It probably is not so easy to just go and find yourself a Swedish lover – but it certainly helps if you can!

LYNN'S SNAPSHOT

He'd been my university sweetheart. We got together again 20 years later but he finished it after 10 years, only because I asked for a decision as I knew it was going wrong.

He broke my heart. Even more so because six months later he took up with someone who was about 16 years younger than him, married her as she was pregnant and then had an affair with his first wife.

I was depressed for about a year and could hardly operate. I resigned my job and stayed in most of the time.

I was unable to play music in the house after we split up and it is only now, after seven years, that I have started playing the odd track.

My best friend was truly wonderful, taking me out with her very new boyfriend every Saturday to make sure that I at least saw the outside world.

From that relationship I learnt never, ever to try and make it up. We went off for a weekend in France four months after the split – it was idyllic, until it dawned on me that he saw it just as a spree in France and not a means to a reconciliation.

It was only when I realised that he had started seeing this ex-employee of his – and when one of his friends told me they were getting married – that I made the momentous effort (spurred on by my dad) to totally change my world.

I went to work in a wildlife hospital in Greece. This liberated me. One morning while cycling to the bakery to get stale bread for the injured birds, sweeping down a hillside with the sun on my back and my nostrils filled with the scent of thyme, I realised that I could operate on my own.

But even now, seven years on, I still wonder about him. One of his friends is in touch with me and he has very gently made me realise that the man I knew was in fact partly made up by my own imagination.

I also learnt to take a reality check of any relationship – not just live it in the mind. It's so important to see it for what it is, warts and all.

John's story

Age at marriage: 22
Age at break-up: 25

Any children?

No, luckily

What was the cause of the split?

We were just not able to live with each other any more. It was a mutual realisation but I had the final call.

What efforts did you make individually or as a couple to save the marriage?

We did a very great deal of talking to family members, which wasn't easy for me as they were in the UK and I was living in Sydney, and of course just trying and trying to find a solution to our incompatibility.

If you turned to professionals, in what ways did they help?

She had a slightly troubled history and the counsellor and the therapist only wanted to see her. I can't be sure they helped in any way.

How did you sort out the finances?

Being so young we didn't have much. We just wrote out assets on paper and it was a fairly easy split. At the time, I thought I would be moving back to the UK so gave her virtually every-thing, like the car and all household belongings.

How were you affected, emotionally and physically, by the split?

It hurt. I hate having the divorce tag over my name for ever now. I was also extremely embarrassed among family and friends that we had broken up so soon after our marriage.

It has left me feeling very concerned and worried about moving further forward with my current girlfriend.

How did you cope when you were living alone?

My good friend Adam went through the exact same thing so it was helpful to follow his guidance. The thing I noticed the most post-marriage was the amount of money I saved and so quickly. I have been able to put thousands behind me now and buy myself so much. I have also travelled extensively world-wide.

Would you have done anything differently?

No. I can happily and honestly say this without passing any blame. The only thing I could have done was live with her for a good while before deciding whether or not to get married.

How long did it take to put your life back together, or at least to feel like facing the world?

A year, I'd say. But it's taken about two to three to get over it. It still hurts to think of what I went through and why it all happened and would it have been better if we hadn't married. I no longer miss her or have feelings for her or the relationship, just insecurities over my ability to maintain a decent relationship now.

How has your life evolved since the break-up?

I have built up an entirely new friendship base and I have never been as happy as I am now.

I've started running marathons and doing long-distance endurance sports, which means I travel widely and meet all sorts of interesting people. I'm running my own business as a personal trainer and it's going really well.

I have such a great life now that I no longer want to return to the UK.

Any advice for others?

- Don't marry unless you've spent several years in a relationship and definitely live together first, for at least a year.

- Listen to your mum – as long as she's as great as mine!

Kate's story

Age at marriage: 23
Age at break-up: 30

Any children?

No

What was the cause of the split?

I came from a very religious family and so was totally inexperienced sexually when I married. If my husband and I had lived together during our two-year courtship then I would have known that we were not sexually compatible, even though we were totally compatible in all other ways.

I reached the age of 30 and simply couldn't face staying in a platonic relationship for my next decade. I had avoided starting a family for the same reasons. I guess I knew I'd never be able to cope with it for ever although I was brought up to believe that the honourable course of action was in fact to do just that and that the really selfish thing would be to put my own needs first.

I had also become very close (but never in a physical way) to a guy at work and became more focused on work and chatting to him. It was clear we could have developed this into something really fantastic – and so it proved to be when I married him at 32 and we had seven excellent years until he died.

What efforts did you make individually or as a couple to save the marriage?

None. I spent at least a year wrestling with my conscience and then made the decision to part from my husband. The last thing I wanted was to try to save the marriage as it had been so inappropriate from the beginning.

I was never able to tell the truth to my husband. I felt it would be too unkind to tell him that things had never been right for me. Instead I lied and said that I had changed. This was a mistake as he then wanted to try marriage guidance. I wouldn't agree to do this as I just knew that what was missing could never be put right.

With hindsight the whole business of telling this lie was a mistake and very spineless, although my motivation had been to spare him as much pain as I could.

If you turned to professionals in what ways did they help?
I didn't seek help. Neither of us did.

How did you sort out the finances?
As my husband was from a moneyed background, my solicitor advised me how I could get maximum money from the house, the savings and the property portfolio, all of them my husband's.

I am glad to say I had the decency to ignore this advice. Instead, as my husband had bought our house outright when we married and there was no mortgage (but I had worked full-time) I suggested we have the house valued and we then split the difference between what he had paid for it and what it was then worth. I kept the savings I had earned for myself and took nothing from the house in terms of possessions, although he insisted I took the cooker which had been a wedding gift from my parents. I returned some valuable diamond jewellery which had been in his family but at his insistence kept my engagement ring.

A month afterwards, our jointly held premium bond came up and we won £25. My husband sent me a cheque for £12.50 and a very pleasant letter, under the circumstances. I felt I'd at least done the right thing in terms of the money aspect of it all.

How were you affected, emotionally and physically, by the split?

I was very, very, sad to think that because of my inexperience at the time, I had made a totally wrong move in marrying him, and so caused him much pain for several years.

I continued to blame myself for my selfishness. I had always believed I was a good person and I had to face up to knowing more about myself – and not being proud of it. I worked through this, however, and realised much more about myself, and life in general, in the process. I feel I did the right thing, and have become more sensitive to others and their perceived failings as a result. I think I'm a nicer person now and can be of more help to my family, friends and others. I feel this process could have so easily gone wrong and I know that if it had then I might never have recovered.

How did you cope when you were living alone?

I was free to begin seeing the guy at work who became my husband two years later, and so I guess there was not a lot of coping to do. There was much more to do when he in turn died, leaving me with two little girls.

Would you have done anything differently?

Nothing at all. I know that if we'd lived together before marrying none of this might have happened, so I have always been relieved that both my daughters are living with their partners and are in no great hurry to marry.

How long did it take to put your life back together, or at least to feel like facing the world?

I suppose about a year, but the real agonising was done before I acted – something I'd strongly recommend. There were only feelings of guilt and self-loathing to tackle. He had, I felt, never done anything except do his best to give me everything – even put me on a pedestal a bit – and I had repaid this by putting myself first and this was hard to come to terms with.

There were strategies that helped me: being certain the path I was on was the right one and keeping busy from day to day at work. Talking was important, too, with my close friends, who I suspect I burdened but I know they were glad to help. Also, learning to forgive myself and even like myself again.

How has your life evolved since the break-up?

My ex read my husband's death notice in the local paper and contacted me to see if I was OK. In fact he offered to live with or even remarry me but with no physical demands (meaning separate rooms). He just felt I'd need money and security and someone to be a friend. That was a very tempting offer at the time but one I had to resist. It showed what a lovely guy he was. I'm really glad he's found someone else and has married again and is happy. I too have a long-term partner and a very happy, fulfilled life.

Any advice for others?

- I relied on friends to get me through this process but would strongly advise anyone to ensure they seek help if needed.

- Think, analyse, visualise possible future scenarios, think of the practicalities, talk to a trusted friend if you can, and then, above all, rely on your own judgement. You have to have self-belief when crises come, simply because in the end, all of us are far more capable of solving our own problems than we can ever imagine.

- Prioritise your own health and wellbeing.

- In the end you have to be true to yourself, and then you can only seek to achieve what you want while always trying to be as kind to the other person as possible. That way you have a chance of coming through it all with some degree of self-worth – eventually.

Andrea's story

Age at marriage: 18
Age at break-up: 23

Any children?

None from that marriage, thankfully

What was the cause of the split?

Incompatibility. My first husband, an Iranian 11 years older than me, took me back to live in his own country and then changed considerably.

He drank heavily, smoked opium and became very violent on occasions. I was a trained ballet dancer but he denied me the chance of dancing with the national ballet company – in case his family found out I had been showing my legs in public – but he let me teach in the national ballet school as that represented an additional income.

While he was in prison for embezzlement I started divorce proceedings, which was a long drawn-out process under Iranian law and meant I had to go into hiding when he was released as he had threatened various methods of harming me, including throwing acid over me.

What efforts did you make individually or as a couple to save the marriage?

I did go back to him on an earlier occasion under pressure from his family, having left him after a particularly violent episode. His promises to reform and stop the violence, however, came to nothing.

If you turned to professionals, in what ways did they help?

I didn't feel I needed counselling or anything, but I secured the services of an Iranian woman solicitor who was brilliant.

How did you sort out the finances?

I left with nothing. It was fortunate we had no children as under Iranian law the father automatically has custody in the event of a divorce.

How were you affected, emotionally and physically, by the split?

During the actual separation before the divorce was finalised, which took several months, I was constantly terrified that he would find me. I was not allowed to leave the country without his permission and various contingency plans were considered, including smuggling me into Afghanistan or getting me down to the Persian Gulf where my father was working.

My eyesight suffered and I suddenly found I needed glasses, which according to the optician was stress-related.

Would you have done anything differently?

No.

How did you cope when you were living alone?

I moved countries, found work and relied on a great network of supportive friends.

I was very happy to put the whole experience behind me, which I was able to do by moving right away and with the help of very good friends and a new relationship.

How long did it take to put your life back together or at least to feel like facing the world?

I started doing that while the divorce was going through.

How your life has evolved since the break-up?

I am now married and have three sons, so that whole episode is long behind me. I still have strong connections with Iran and indeed with the family of my ex-husband, but I have not seen him since the divorce.

Any advice for others?

- Don't be pressured to stay in a relationship that's not working, particularly if there is an element of violence.

- Look forward without regret.

- When I was very low at one point, an Iranian friend pointed out all the millions of people worse off than me and that has helped me ever since whenever I feel a little down about things.

EMMA'S SNAPSHOT

He was young enough to be my son. I was in my forties and he was in his twenties. He was African and we'd met in India. We were in a relationship for four years, three-and-a-half of them living together.

He introduced me to music, culture, a life that I had never experienced before. He also cost me a fortune as he managed to persuade me to spend most of my savings on him.

He's never known my true age. He thought I was 10 years older than him, certainly not 23 years older, and I never disabused him. I lost all touch with reality. I found out about his total lack of faithfulness and I was devastated when I finally chucked him out.

But my best friend was there for me and took me to comedy clubs and concerts.

Looking back, I can only think 'Poor man, look at the age difference, who can blame him?'

He apologised to me many months later and has kept in touch by phone. He can still make me giggle and feel irrepressibly carefree. He is now married with twins – one of whom he has called a name remarkably similar to my nickname.

Jenny's story

Age at marriage:18
Age at break-up: 42

Any children?

A son aged 23

What was the cause of the split?

I'd suffered 26 years of physical, sexual and mental abuse and infidelity. I attempted suicide on two occasions and was hospitalised. It was my decision to end the marriage.

What efforts did you make individually or as a couple to save the marriage?

I suggested that we should go for counselling and that he should seek some kind of help with his behaviour, but as far as he was concerned the marriage was OK. He would say it was my fault that he behaved like he did; if I did what he told me to do he wouldn't get angry with me and I wouldn't get beaten. I had nowhere to go and no money.

If you turned to professionals, in what ways did they help?

He was in the Army at the time and they were just not interested in helping. They had the same attitude as the police, which was not to get involved with domestic situations. Nowadays, I am sure you can turn to the unit welfare officer who will help and put you in touch with the right organisation.

The first time my case went to court it was thrown out because they said there wasn't enough evidence to support my claim of my husband's abuse. After six months I changed to another solicitor who wasn't much better. He told me the only way I was going to get my divorce was to admit to adultery.

I was seeing somebody at the time, but I had not committed adultery with him. After a couple of months he said to me: "What the hell, if it means you can get your divorce and get rid of this chap, admit to it. I don't mind being cited."

How did you sort out the finances?

As far as finances and the home were concerned, I had no say in the matter. My husband told me what I was going to get and if I didn't accept his offer of half the proceeds of the house I would end up with nothing. Everything was in his name.

My solicitor said I would be better off accepting his offer because if it turned nasty my husband could move the money offshore and I would end up with nothing.

How were you affected, emotionally and physically, by the split?

I wasn't affected by the split – I have no regrets at all about that – but I was deeply affected by the marriage.

I have been scarred mentally. I still get flashbacks and I wake up in the middle of the night crying because of nightmares. I can't watch any TV programmes that show violence towards women.

At the time it was all happening I had nowhere to go or any money and I didn't know of any women's refuge. But I am now at the stage of life where it doesn't bother me any more. I think the only anger I have, if anger is the right word, is that I did not get the money that was due to me and that he bragged to his new wife how lucky he was to have got out of the marriage so lightly seeing that he had committed adultery so many times and treated me so badly.

How did you cope when you were living alone?

I walked for a whole day looking for somewhere to live. I eventually found a house that had a little flat in the attic. I can remember sitting in the middle of the room and thinking 'This will do, I am safe here and it is mine. I can now decide who I let in and I can do what I want, when I want.' It was a turning point in my life – there was now light at the end of the tunnel.

I really coped very well. I was strengthened by the knowledge that I had done the best thing I could possibly do. It was such a relief to get out of that relationship.

Would you have done anything differently?

Knowing what I know now I would certainly have gone to the police early on and stuck by my accusations and then tried to make a life for myself and my child. I only stayed with my husband as long as I did because of my son, who I felt needed both of us. I realise now you don't need a man in your life to bring up a child. If you give it the right amount of love and there are male relatives who the child can look up to, the child will grow up well balanced.

How long did it take to put your life back together, or at least to feel like facing the world?

About a year. Once I was out of his grasp and control the world seemed a much better place. I had space to think clearly.

How has your life evolved since the break-up?

I am now in a happy, stable relationship with a man who worships the ground that I walk on. He has built up my confidence which has enabled me to retrain as a nurse and over the past five years encouraged me to go back into adult education, and that has boosted my ego no end.

Any advice for others?

- Don't stay in an abusive relationship just for the sake of the children.

- Don't be frightened to ask for help. You are not a punchbag for anybody just because the person has issues.

- Seek advice. There are plenty of organisations that can help.

- Don't think you are alone.

- Go to the police and don't back down. No one has the right to beat their partner no matter what problems you may have.

JO'S SNAPSHOT

My marriage ended after 18 years, to my great surprise. My husband met someone though a lonely hearts advert in the local paper. He lied to her and said he was divorced so when they met and fell in love he was a bit desperate to get out of our marriage.

She was divorced and childless – almost like an open invitation to my husband, who was presumably flattered that she seemed to fancy him.

It all careered ahead quite rapidly, with a few months of subterfuge and deceit followed by his admission and then his terrifying bouts of violent anger towards me (presumably because I wasn't 'her').

I couldn't bear being under the same roof as him because the atmosphere was so painful. You could almost feel my despair and his fury reverberating round the house. I had to get away so, against all the best advice, I took my children, then aged 16 and 13, to a tiny cottage I'd managed to rent – just far enough away for me to be independent of my soon-to-be ex but close enough for the children to continue their school and social lives.

Moving was cathartic. I immediately felt better. I remember touching, almost caressing, every wall in that cottage, thinking "This is mine – he can't get at me now." The children appreciated the peaceful end to a bad period and were very close and supportive to me while remaining loyal and loving to their dad.

The move was the first and most important step I took in putting my life back together. It gave me an immediate fresh start as well as independence and courage. I coped with everything myself – the house purchase, the mortgage, all the financial issues, the whole lot. I liked knowing that I could stand on my own two feet – something that, as a married person, you have no idea that you can do.

Six months after moving out and starting my new life I changed my name by deed poll. I'd always used my maiden name for work anyway, so officially becoming that person again meant a lot to me. I talked it over with the children first, because I didn't want them to think I was trying to dissociate myself from them, and they both said 'Don't blame you. Go for it.' So I did. It meant a lot to me.

CHANGING YOUR NAME

One way to shake off the old you, if you're a woman, is to revert to your maiden name. No longer being Mrs Get-the-hell-out-of-my-life could be important to you as you take up the mantle of an independent life. So, if you're not happy about remaining saddled with the moniker of your ex, and you fancy using your old family name again, you have a choice:

You can use your decree absolute and marriage certificate or, if this method is not accepted as documentary evidence, you can change your name by deed poll.

If you take the latter option it is not necessary to wait until your divorce. You have the right to change your surname at any time while you are separated. The fee for an adult deed poll is £34 for online or postal applications, £39 by phone or in person [see box at end of chapter].

Duncan's story

Age at time of marriage: 21
Age at time of break-up: 29

Any children?
No children, thankfully

What was the cause of the split?

We had the same problem running through the duration of the marriage. I think it was just a case of poor communication which led to the break-up. I met someone in April last year and realised I had feelings for them, which was worrying since I was supposed to be happily married. Before I could let anything happen with this other person I told my wife that I thought it best we split up.

What efforts did you make individually or as a couple to save the marriage?

When I first told her, my wife suggested we go to marriage guidance counselling. I refused as I thought that regardless of what we would discuss I had reached a point where I felt that I could not continue in the relationship.

A couple of weeks later, after she had moved out, I thought I had made a mistake and asked if we could try to make a go of things. For a month, while she was still back living with her parents 25 miles away, we went out at weekends, I cooked her meals and tried to show her that I still loved her. About three weeks into this, the same things which made me unhappy in the first place started to come out again.

Therefore, a month after we'd decided to make a go of it, I said that it would be for the best if we made the split permanent, and she agreed.

If you turned to professionals, in what ways did they help?

We didn't seek outside help, but we are doing our divorce online. I saw a solicitor at the outset, as I never thought I would be in a position where we would get divorced. It was as expected, quite intimidating, but I got the information I needed.

How did you sort out the finances?

We managed to sort everything out quite amicably. We agreed to divide all the debts 50-50, and despite getting a crazy letter from her regarding the furniture, where she had put values on everything (for example, a metal bed I was using which was broken, she valued at £200) we managed to sort things out in a relatively pain-free way.

We sold the house, which we had just bought, and got everything in the financial consent ready for the divorce.

In the end I got most of the electrical equipment, stereo, DVD recorder and so on, while she took the fridge-freezer, sofas, coffee tables and things like that. I wasn't really too fussed as I would prefer to buy my own new furniture which had no attachment to the old relationship.

How were you affected, emotionally and physically, by the split?

For me, being the one who made the decision, it was odd. I've never broken up with anyone in my life, so the first time was my wife. The first three months passed in a complete blur, where no day really stood out. I wondered whether I had made the right decision. Insomnia was dreadful: I would go to bed at one or two in the morning, and wake up between three and four and then not be able to get back to sleep.

However, I used the time constructively. I started to eat better, do regular exercise and get back in contact with my friends and family. I had spent so much time in an insular environment when I was married that it seemed nothing existed outside of it.

I drank more, but only when I was going out with my mates, never on my own. The hardest times were things like her birthday, our anniversary and Christmas. But now I've been through them all on my own it's no longer a case of 'a year ago we were ...'

I've changed as a person. I refuse to settle for second best any more and am a lot more choosy about anyone that I would consider being in a relationship with. I've learnt patience as well.

Now, nearly a year since we finally split, I find myself thinking of her less and I feel better in every way. I feel free.

How did you cope when you were living alone?

My wife always did the washing and things like that, even though I always offered, or if I did do them she would redo everything, saying it wasn't up to standard. Before we met I had lived on my own for two years so I slipped back into it quite easily. If anything, I enjoyed it as I was looking after myself.

I ate better food and at a sensible time. It was difficult when we finally split, living in the house we had just bought. It was to have been the start of us having our own family, so it reminded me of everything that was no more – especially when she started seeing someone where we worked together a fortnight after we split.

In the end I went and lived with my mum for three months, which was just what I needed as I was out of that house and with my mum who I get on with really well. Without her support I would not have dealt with things as well as I did.

Would you have done anything differently?

Hindsight is a wonderful thing, and I'm not an 'if only' kind of chap. However, looking back now, I think we just took advantage of each other. We loved each other, for sure, but I don't think we gave each other what we actually needed. I should have taken the time and trouble to listen more, and not just listen, but *listen*. Men and women communicate verbally in different ways and I should have taken the time to just be there for her more. I like to think that I can solve anything but I learnt that sometimes you don't need to solve it, you just need to shut up, listen and then give them a hug.

I also should have made more effort to make her feel special. I think after a while we both neglected each other and I know that I could have done a lot more.

We just needed to be more honest with each other, talk more about stuff that mattered to us and just made the other person feel like we did when we first met and when we got married.

How long did it take to put your life back together, or at least to feel like facing the world again?

I was ready to face the world from day one and just a few months down the line I was able to do it in a better, more focused way. I am still putting my life back together, but the difference is that what I'm doing now is fine tuning. The first three months when this happened was when it was the total overhaul, questioning myself and so on.

During that time I had loads of weird thoughts; for example, I thought that as I had inflicted so much hurt on someone I loved, that I would also have the same hurt, but in a different way – a kind of cosmic karma or something.

In total it probably took about seven months to come to terms with things, accept what I had done, and get used to my new life.

How has your life evolved since the break-up?

When I moved in with my mum I gave myself 100 days to sort

everything out, and then I would move back to the place that had been 'our town'. I managed it in 99 days. I bought new furniture, even a new bed, and was renting a two-bedroom flat right in the centre of town.

The first five weeks were hard, but I slowly got used to living on my own and in the end absolutely loved it. I could come home after work, close the door and do whatever I wanted. My mates could come round, and being so close to town came in handy staggering back after nights out.

In due course I decided that it would be best if I left town so I could get a proper new start for myself and my soon-to-be ex-wife could get on with her life with her new bloke without me being around.

So I got a new job a long way away. Sure, there are still some times when I miss her, but I think that's because we were together for so long and I got used to having someone that close to me always around (especially since we also worked in the same place).

I enjoy my life now, more than when I was married. I've learnt things about myself and understood some of the things that I should have done when we were married which may have made me feel differently, and also made her happier.

I'm now 30, living 80 miles away from the place I was born and lived in for ten years of my life, which included our entire married life. I am so much closer to my mum and brother that I feel lucky in a way that I was given the chance to build some bridges and show them both that I can be reliable.

I've become an uncle for the first time, which is cool. I don't come from a big or close family, so for me to have a relationship with my mum, my brother, his wife and their kids, makes me feel lucky. I realised that I would like to be a dad at some point in my life but if it doesn't happen, then it doesn't happen.

Also, there have been some mates of mine who have really helped me get through it. My mate Dan was always there, especially at the beginning, to take me to the pub and make me look at things logically when I was angry and frustrated.

Another friend, Dee, who is also getting divorced, has been ace. I'm like a big brother to her and she is like a little sister to me. We just look out for each other and try to support each other when we have bad days.

Lou is another one who has helped, always being there for me, especially as she worked in the same place, so when things were getting weird there she was someone I could just vent my spleen to and she'd listen.

This entire thing has shown me who my real friends are, that I'm not really that bad a person, and that my family mean a lot to me. While I am not yet the person I want to be, I am slowly getting there, with their help.

Any advice for others?

- Use the time to work out who you are and what you want to be. Sure you may have just come out of a relationship with someone, but there is only one person you live with 24/7, and that's you. No one you ever meet will spend as much time with you as yourself. And you need to be happy with who you are, otherwise you will tear yourself apart, with 'if only I'd done did this' and so on.

- Just hang on in there when it happens. Days, weeks and months all merge into one at first and it can be very disconcerting. Make a routine and stick to it: even if it is as boring as hell, with your life in utter chaos you need something to fall back on.

- Talk to people. Mates and family are different though. My mum, having been through divorce herself, and the fact that she's my mum, would listen to me going on for hours about this. Mates will be like this at the beginning but after a while, their interest will wane, not because you're boring them but because they have their own issues to deal with.

STEPHEN'S SNAPSHOT

When everything fell apart, my first instinct was to go back to my parents' home. Practically and emotionally I needed somewhere I felt secure. I had no illusions that it would be an easy option; they live a long way away and news of my break-up came as a total shock to them. So there were plenty of questions to answer and I started building up my own defence, casting myself as the victim because I was fearful they would reject me and I'd be completely alone. I needn't have done that. Whatever their thoughts about my situation, they are my family and they put aside their judgement to listen to me and give me the time to go through all that happened.

It was odd to be home, surrounded by echoes of my childhood, of life before my marriage. In some ways this was the best way to start my own healing process, but it was also an unreal environment in which food was always on the table, my washing was done and I had no immediate financial worries.

As days turned into weeks I started to realise that not only was I holding back the inevitable realities of everyday life, I was also stopping my own family from dealing with their thoughts and fears about the marriage breakdown. My sullen presence was a constant reminder to them that something awful had happened. Though no one ever asked me to go I knew that being at my parents' home needed to be a temporary crutch, not a long-term plan.

Jennifer's story

Age at marriage: 26
Age at break-up: 40

Any children?

One daughter aged eight

What was the cause of the split?

I got cancer at 40 and consequently was going through a period when I contemplated an early death. I realised my marriage was a comfortable friendship, but not much more. I also realised I had been, from the start, living the life my husband wanted to live and not my life. Because of him I was then living in Australia – I did not want to be there. If I was told I had six months to live, what would I do? Answer: I would leave my marriage and go and live in England.

I was told I had an 80/20 chance of survival, but the hard thinking could not be put aside. I knew I didn't want to die regretting the things I had never done.

What efforts did you make individually or as a couple to save the marriage?

None, to be honest. My husband was bewildered. He did not understand what was happening or why. To complicate matters further I had also decided that I might be capable of having a sexual relationship with another woman. I realised about that same time that I had been falling in love with women all my life. I now wanted to find out if my emotions would lead me into a physical relationship. But this was not information I wanted to share with my husband. I did not want a custody battle over our daughter and I did not think that my husband would either understand or respect my new choices.

We agreed to separate for six months and I travelled to England with our daughter. At the end of that time my husband visited the UK. We saw each other briefly. I then told him that the marriage was over.

If you turned to professionals in what ways did they help?
Neither of us sought help.

How were you affected, emotionally and physically, by the split?
Guilt still haunts me. The decision to break the marriage was mine; the responsibility for the separation and break-up was mine. My husband never understood what happened. The break hit him like a meteor strike. It came from nowhere. I think that for many years he mourned losing me.

How did you sort out the financial and residence issues?
We had sold our house just before the break-up and I suggested we split everything, house, money and shares, 50-50 and my ex agreed. Most of what we divided I had inherited from my mother.

My ex did not offer any financial support for our daughter. I thought he should provide some level of support, but it was a battle and took more than two years to get him to agree a minimal level. I did not involve courts.

I hoped he would telephone or email our daughter often, but he did not communicate with her very much. He sometimes forgot birthdays and she was very hurt and upset by this and his continuing attitude of reluctant acknowledgment of his role makes it hard for her to believe he loves her.

How were you affected, emotionally and physically, by the break-up?

I think there is still a lot I have never dealt with. The guilt is buried deep inside like shrapnel and I do not propose to dig it out.

How did you cope when you were living alone?

I went with my daughter from the marital home to live with friends 12,000 miles away in England – a household with a lesbian couple, two teenagers, one 80-year-old man, two cats and three dogs. We stayed there for two years before I bought a flat and moved to live there with my daughter.

Work was a crucial part of the process of coping. So too were friends. I was fortunate in having only one child and having the financial means to be independent.

Would you have done anything differently?

No, not really, except perhaps I should have seen years earlier that the marriage was not what I wanted. But I was raised by a single-parent mother and I wanted very much to give my daughter a two-parent family.

How long did it take to put your life back together, or at least to feel like facing the world?

It didn't take very long at all. This was because my life went in a different direction – in a real sense of moving so far away from the marriage, and in other ways too, notably sexually and emotionally. The toughest thing for women is often being able to claim their own lives. It was so for me once. I thought first of my husband and my child and always put their needs and wants above my own. But when faced with the prospect of death I realised that I also had a responsibility to myself. I did not want deathbed regrets and so I chose to break free.

I was lucky that I was given a chance for a new life. I was lucky too that I could make that choice. I had the money and the earning power to be free. Many women do not.

How has your life evolved since the break-up?

I went through a period of promiscuity in my 40s and then, at the end of that decade, entered a relationship which has proved nurturing in every way. If I had not stepped out of my routine rut of marriage this new relationship – now almost 13 years old – would never have happened.

Any advice for others?

- Be selfish, in the best sense of the word.
- Live to the full the one life you have.

MILLIE'S SNAPSHOT

The big break-up which rocked my life happened when I was 23. We met at art college and were in an intense relationship for three-and-a-half years.

He was Asian, very handsome, very swamped by family pressures and expectations and like no one I had ever met before. We ignored all the differences between us and he ran away from his family and lived with me for a while during my last year at college. We thought we were being grown-up and moving our relationship forward when really it was completely the wrong thing to do.

With all the external factors to cope with, such as his strict religious upbringing and the intolerable interference of his parents and wider family, the relationship was doomed. We were too young to be able to cope with so much pressure and it turned what should have just been fun into something quite frightening and emotionally fraught.

We both knew it was getting more and more impossible so we finished it in the worst way possible – on the phone. So many things were left unsaid but I think by that stage we'd both had enough.

I was very upset for a while and felt a deep sadness that after everything we had experienced together it had to finish so sourly.

From time to time I'd feel the need to wallow in the past and look at old photos, which was upsetting and did nothing to help my recovery.

It took me well over a year to get over it properly and to feel that I was free of him. I learnt to live with it and I don't have any negative feelings about it now at all. It's a passage of my life that I moved on from and have learnt from in a positive way. I thank my lucky stars we didn't run off and get married, which had been a temptation when he felt cornered by his parents.

My friends were a huge support to me. Most had witnessed our relationship throughout college and afterwards and knew the whole story and what he was like, so I had a great support network wanting me to get my life back on track after the relationship had taken up so much of my time. My dear mum was also instrumental in picking me up and dusting me down – very supportive and wise.

I didn't have a problem getting on with my life once I'd moved to London and started a new career. I also found it much easier to put the past behind me when I made new friends who had no connection with him and that part of my recent past.

EXTRA HELP

For changing names: the UK Deed Poll Service 0800 7833048 www.ukdps.co.uk

CHAPTER 6

Finding someone new

I stopped harbouring any feelings of anger or hate and realised I'd got over the break-up when I entered a new relationship. *Tanya*

Do you sometimes think that if only you could fall in love again everything would be all right? Well, the chances are that you will, especially if you're a man. Men are apparently more likely to remarry than women, according to the 2005 survey by the Yorkshire Building Society when it questioned 3,515 divorced adults about the impact of their marital break-up.

Despite what they may have gone through the first time round, four per cent of men (and two per cent of women) remarried within two years.

Two or more years later, 15% of the men had remarried, but only five per cent of women had. More of the women said they were not interested in a new relationship, preferring to live together or simply date.

The expert says...

Men, in particular, are inclined to seek a new partner before they're properly prepared for a fresh start. They are content to take the option of just papering over the cracks.

Ariana Gee, relationship coach

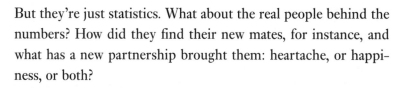

But they're just statistics. What about the real people behind the numbers? How did they find their new mates, for instance, and what has a new partnership brought them: heartache, or happiness, or both?

Many of the answers are here, in this chapter's case studies. For some of the people it has worked wonderfully, for others it's not been so great and they have found themselves coping with a second break-up.

One way to try and make sure you get it right is to prepare yourself properly. This doesn't necessarily mean getting a haircut or buying new shoes before you go out looking for a mate, it means preparing yourself mentally and emotionally for this very important stage of your life. Once again, as with so many aspects of life post-marriage breakdown, it's about taking responsibility for yourself.

Become a successful single first

Trisha Stone is a singles coach, someone who helps people navigate their own lives. She helps them to 'read the map' initially so they know the way they're going and what they want to aim at and how to build the steps into their lives to ensure they get there.

Trisha advises clients that they need to become a successful single before or while they are looking for a relationship. 'Successful' translates as having a full and interesting life and engaging with things that interest you. "When you are leading an authentic life as a single person you are much more likely to meet your partner," she says.

"For a lot of people it's an enormous shock becoming single

again," Trisha adds. "It happened to me. I had to ask myself what I wanted to be and how I wanted to live my life.

"I work with people to build a vision of the life that they want to live. That may include relationships but it's much more important to look at the rest of their lives. I get them to do some of the head stuff, some of the conscious stuff, before their heart engages or they get excited and the hormones start jumping around when they meet somebody who is very attractive to them, because that tends to overshadow things. In that sense we are all the same, whatever age we are.

"A lot of people don't learn a lesson from the past and jump from the frying pan into the fire. We look at the pattern of past relationships and begin to build some boundaries around what you would find acceptable and non-acceptable in a relationship."

Red warning flags

"I talk about people having their antennae up. This means they recognise their red warning flags very early in a relationship and don't repeat a pattern of, say, abuse. They may have ignored their red flags before, but now they are aware when the flags are telling them 'this is not right, this is not good'.

"I can never give people any guarantees of when they will meet that person but after they have done the work they feel far more confident in going out and becoming the chooser in the relationship.

"This is something that is very unusual for women and really changes their perspective – that they choose, too. It's not about being the one who goes out there more than the men do, not about having an aggressive male attitude to it, but it's about being con-

scious of what you're choosing, why you're choosing that particular person and what you're looking for and then being strategic
about it. Ideally, you want both people being the chooser. Both
knowing what they want and finding it in the other person.

"In the past women have been passive, or maybe thought they
were choosing but it wasn't what they really needed in a relationship. I work with my clients through this thing called
Requirements, Needs and Wants.

REQUIREMENTS are the absolutely non-negotiable things in a
relationship that becomes your sort of checklist. It is not cold-
hearted or clinical, it's about staying conscious of what you need.
People are self-revealing and you can find out an enormous
amount about people in a very short period of time.

If you come up against one of your things that is non-negotiable
then don't get into a relationship with that person hoping that
that thing will change because it probably won't. If you see those
signs early on you can not commit yourself and therefore save
yourself an enormous amount of emotional investment and
heartache.

NEEDS are the negotiable part. We work very carefully with all of
those to see if they really are negotiable. I'll say to a client if you
really were very attracted to this person and everything was lovely and you felt yourself to be in love with this person, if they
couldn't understand or cope with something that's important to
you would that then be the deal-breaker for you. If it is, then it's
a Requirement, if not then it's a negotiable Need.

WANTS are the icing on the cake. Someone might be crazy about
their garden and growing their own vegetables and would really
like someone to share that with. But it won't make or break the
relationship. They may or may not share an interest in a certain

thing but it's not critical. They may or may not have similar backgrounds.

People tend to think that they have to look for people with similar backgrounds, but what I say is that long-term relationships are based on shared complementary value systems. You need to know how to look for them, how to recognise them and how to know what your own values are, because research has shown that the reason most relationships break down or at least come to crisis point is that the shared values are not compatible.

They are not seeing the world in the same way. Instead of standing on the top of the mountain looking out on the landscape of their lives and contemplating the issues that they have, they are standing on different mountain tops shouting at each other.

Molly's story

Age at marriage: 18
Age at break-up: 38

Any children?
Two: a daughter of 14 and a son of nine

What was the cause of the split?
I had met someone else with whom I was very much in love, so I ended our marriage.

What efforts did you make individually or as a couple to save the marriage?
We had a weekend away without the children to talk about things, but my heart wasn't in it.

If you turned to professionals, in what ways did they help?

My solicitor was helpful and did what he could for me in light of the fact that I felt the situation was my fault as I had left the family home. Although he advised me on what I was entitled to financially, I was willing to accept less so that my husband could still buy a decent house for the children.

How were you affected, emotionally and physically, by the split?

Racked by guilt at what I had done even though I felt it was the right decision. I believed marriage was for life and had made my vows in church so my emotions were in turmoil.

It was very traumatic telling the children, who did not know what was going on. It appeared I was being very selfish at the time.

My parents were devastated and friends could not believe what had happened as I had not talked about the situation except to one or two close friends.

It was extremely hard to collect my son from school as my new partner's former wife was telling people I had taken her children's father away. (Her children were at the same school, swimming clubs and so on.) I tried to remain calm and keep a dignified silence. The town was quite small and it was so difficult avoiding ex-partners.

I also lost a lot of weight.

How did you sort out the financial and residence issues?

Care and control of the children was worked out amicably. Usually courts do not want to split siblings but my son lived with me during the week and with his dad at the weekends, and my daughter remained with her dad. I would call to see her before school and afterwards before he came home.

Finances took longer to settle as he wanted a bigger share of the marital home.

My son seemed to accept the situation more easily as he didn't fully understand what had happened. I tried to keep his routine as normal as possible.

My daughter was at a vulnerable age, being a young teenager, and was extremely upset. She took the separation very hard and would only have minimal contact with me to begin with. Gradually, after some difficult periods, we were able to rebuild our relationship. She is now very close both to me and my husband. Lots of time, patience and love reaped rewards.

Is there anything that you would you have done differently?

I should have listened to my parents when they told me I was too young to get married – but I thought it was the right decision, being quite naïve.

Had I not got married when I did I would have had more opportunity to experience more of life, pursue a career further and broaden my outlook through travel and meeting people.

How did you cope when you were living alone?

I had my new partner for love and support so the fallout from a break-up was not the same for me.

How long did it take for you to get over it, or at least to feel like facing the world?

Although I had a new partner, I was very sad for my ex-husband as until quite recently he had not found a new companion.

How has your life evolved since the break-up?

It has been a few years now since the split but there are still family ramifications to contend with. My brother has never really accepted the situation. However, the children seem to have survived and we get on really well now. As they mature they can see that life does not necessarily turn out how you think it will, even with the best of intentions.

We had lots of support from friends and we met new people who did not know our previous history.

Any advice for others?

- You have to be very strong so consider all the implications before you decide on any action.

- Explore the options of professional advice.

- Be very aware that it's a huge risk to take, especially if you have children. If you are very unhappy then making the break can give a more positive and worthwhile future – we are very fortunate that it has worked for us.

- Imagine how you would like things to be in ten years' time.

GEOFF'S SNAPSHOT

Mine was a 1960s shotgun marriage, doomed to failure. We were teenagers and penniless, and soon became parents, too. It was not the best way to mature into adults.

We grew apart while we did our growing up and, inevitably, our marriage finally fizzled out 22 years later. We were of a generation for whom divorce was a last option, never a first one, but once the children were teenagers (another significant factor in the story of marital stresses, it must be said), my wife and I were living virtually separate lives.

Arguments became routine and a separation of some kind eventually became inevitable: it was just a question of practicalities.

In the end I was the one who took the initiative. I rented a small house and moved out. Our sons, aged 22 and 19, stayed in the family home with my wife.

However, once I had escaped from the crushing, confrontational atmosphere of the family home and realised the sheer joy of living in my own space, I quickly found I had other problems to face: the extraordinarily difficult business of looking after myself. From a practical standpoint, it was extremely testing.

I had never, ever, had to do anything remotely domesticated in my life, having gone from childhood home to marital home overnight, and had no idea how to fend for myself.

I shopped daily, sometimes hourly, because I was terrified of sell-by dates and poisoning myself.

I lived off sandwiches (Safeway – prawn and mayo), takeaways (Indian, Chinese and fish and chips) and microwave meals (Findus Menu Master) for a long time and am now, 20 years on, tackling the cholesterol problems that are the legacy of that disastrous diet. I leant on many friends, friends' wives and relatives to help guide me through the mysteries of the kitchen and the supermarket. I would call them, on a sort of rota basis, for advice on critical issues such as how to heat a pie, how to change a duvet cover (that's quite difficult to comprehend over the telephone) and whether eight minutes was long enough to boil baked beans. This last dilemma was solved for me by the woman who years later bravely took on the responsibility for boiling my baked beans for me (or whatever it is you do to them) when she became my wife.

A WEBSITE FOR MEN

Wifesgone [*details at end of chapter*] is a website created by someone who has himself been through all the practical and emotional difficulties of separation and divorce.

Adrian Hamilton describes his site as "a one-stop-shop to assist men bringing order and quality living back into their single lives".

He adds: "After my own marriage ended I wanted to design a portal to help men reconnect with the world. It can be a very alienating and lonely time and it's important that you look forward and learn about rebuilding your lives from people in a similar situation.

"So many issues suddenly become overwhelming, dealing with the legal issues and costs of divorce, like rebuilding relationships with your children, financial, education, relocation, jobs, holidays – even doing the washing, cooking and cleaning – the list is never-ending on how your life is affected.

"One's concentration and health are affected, feelings of sadness, despair, loneliness and dislocation creep in and it's very hard to know where to turn. With friendships changing as a result of the new situation, many men can feel that they have no one to turn to. That is a very hard place to be at."

Wifesgone has a forum where men can communicate with each other and exchange sources of helpful information on starting a new life.

Malcolm's story

Age at marriage: 26
Age at break-up: 52

Any children?
Two, aged 20 and 18

What was the cause of the split?
My ex is an alcoholic and after trying to get her to stop for 17 years it got to the point where I just couldn't handle it any longer. My heart couldn't give any more. I used to come home from work, clean the house, look after the kids and all the time she'd be passed out.

What efforts did you make individually or as a couple to save the marriage?
I tried to make it work but in the end I gave up, I was beaten. I never again lifted a finger. The house turned into a shameful cesspit. She left of her own accord, leaving me with £23,000 of debt on credit cards and cash drawn from the bank.

If you turned to professionals in what ways did they help?
Our divorce was dealt with by mediation but my ex couldn't keep the appointments because of her drunken state. Again, I gave up in the end. The mediator did what she could and was fair but I still considered the line she took was weighted more in my ex's favour than mine.

How did you sort out the finances?
My ex agreed to my having the house and in return she would receive £10,000. I was to take on all the debt and not claim costs against her. Although this was all agreed between us it was

impossible to get her into court to finalise the settlement. The decree absolute came through three years ago and I didn't even know it! Nobody told me. Since then my ex has come back for more, having blown all her money and once again got herself in £5,000 debt. On top of that she says I've been beating her up and threatening her.

I feel let down by the whole system knowing (so I'm told) that she could still, even six years on, get half of everything and I could become homeless because of it. Meanwhile she sits pretty in her house that the state pays for, raking in benefits and anything else that's going. All I want is a clean break, but I can't find anyone who can help me achieve that without it costing me a fortune – which I don't have.

The kids don't speak to her unless they have to as they're disgusted by the way she lies so freely.

How were you affected, emotionally and physically, by the split?

By the time she finally left my love for her was burnt out. I just had nothing left to give. The day she went I felt elated – a huge weight had been lifted from my heart, though possibly not from hers.

She is a very vindictive type of person and always thinks she's right, even when it can be proved she isn't. That makes life very hard for anyone to cope with. It was a relief for me to no longer have things thrown at me and to be punched and sworn at continually.

How did you cope when you were living alone?

Being alone wasn't that much of a worry. I now feel that after all the years of having to do everything I have earned the right to run my own life, and I can do that very well as I'm a good cook and I can even knit and sew. I acquired these skills early in life as I'd played an important role in the family house after my father was murdered.

When my ex left me, she cleared out the house, taking every single thing except the light bulbs and the fridge. I managed for two years with just deckchairs and a cheap picnic table in the house and slept on an airbed before I could start to afford things. I gradually improved the house, month by month, finally completing it last year with a kitchen that I fitted myself.

I have at times become very depressed and have sat and had a good cry. In fact I still do, many times, trying to get my head round all the debt and the way I'm having to live my life.

For six years I've worked a 16-hour day at my job as a phone repair engineer and doing cleaning work at night to clear the debt.

Twice in that time I've collapsed at work and been rushed to hospital. I was told I was suffering from severe exhaustion on top of a heart attack and now I've just had a mild stroke as well. All in all, the stress and worry will probably get me long before I get what the state owes me as a pension.

Would you have done anything differently?

No, even after this whole disaster. And I would still get married again. There's nothing wrong with marriage if both partners work together.

How long did it take to put your life back together, or at least to feel like facing the world?

I think the fact I was working helped immensely as at least I had people around me. Even though I wasn't always able to talk to them it was still company, and it was the same when I was cleaning at night.

But it's been the internet that's been my main lifeline as a place to meet people and talk to them. Mind you, it was a pain trying to find sites where people didn't swear. I only became brave enough to do this when I decided that I didn't have to live alone and I went on to a dating site – though even here I actually came across women who were incredibly vain and were looking for an easy life with a big house and lots of spending money. It was amazing to be asked what my income was, as if that's any basis for a friendship.

How has your life evolved since the break-up?

There have been many times in the past six years when I've had no food in the house for two or three days at a time. There'd be only water to drink and I would eat the leftover sandwiches when meetings were held at work. A few years back one of the directors sat me down and asked me what was wrong. After I told him he gave me a bit of a telling-off but then he and his wife came round every week to see me and bring basic food for me, like porridge, long-life milk and potatoes. This went on until he was killed in an air crash, the company was sold and we were all made redundant.

Since then I have had to survive as best I can as no permanent jobs have come up and I'm not entitled to any state help at all. I've tried to get help from all sorts of places, even the Red Cross, but they all tell me they don't give food to the likes of me, only to organisations. As a result of this I no longer give anything to any charity. If I'm asked, I'm afraid they get told very firmly why.

Once I'd sort of given myself 'permission' to seek friendship among the opposite sex and I was exploring internet dating sites, I felt I was living again. Through this I met a lady last year and we are so much alike it's amazing. She has also gone through a bad divorce, only her kids were young when it happened. She knows about the difficulties I'm in and has helped as much as she can. She knows I can't treat her to any luxuries and it seems she is OK about that. We are both very good cooks and that's something we enjoy doing together.

I went into this without expecting to be making love at every opportunity but just to be happy to sit together, in silence if necessary. I want my new lady to know she is loved and thought about, so I tell her that. I often like to step up behind her and slip my arms around her and kiss her and hug her. We do this to each other, even though she's not tall enough to reach my neck! It's lovely. My ex used to push me away and tell me to f*** off.

Any advice for others?

- Bear with it – it does get better over time.

- Getting over any feelings of blame, guilt and hatred is an important step on your way to recovery.

- Don't make the mistake of going for another partner on the rebound of a bad relationship. It causes more pain, so give it time.

- Look after your health and your appearance as best you can.

- Living alone doesn't mean you have to become a couch potato. An hour's walking is good for you, even with the kids, and it costs nothing.

Internet dating

This has been one of the most significant changes to influence the lives of single people since a blind date brought Adam and Eve together in the Garden of Eden.

Being able to make friends with people right around the globe, and to flirt with them from the comfort of your computer chair while eating toast and wearing your slippers, is a giant leap for mankind's lovelorn and lonely – and the just plain curious.

Where once it was quite normal to meet your potential mate at work, in a bar, a nightclub or through friends, nowadays it is just as likely that the internet will be responsible for firing off Cupid's arrow. And there's no stigma attached to it. Quite the opposite, in fact, as more and more people of every social class and background take themselves off into the ether to track down their perfect other half.

But be warned: It's not so much a jungle out there as an ocean, with a disturbing number of sharks waiting to make a meal out of the unwary. Take risks, fall for flattering lies and deceit, and you may put yourself at risk.

Observe the rules and use common sense and you should be fine.

The expert says...

I think it is important, if you are interested in someone, to work very quickly towards meeting them as soon as possible. Too many people get carried away exchanging emails and talking on the phone, and they believe they're in a relationship when really they're not. Then when they finally get to meet the person it is often a great disappointment.

I know of one woman who was spending three hours a night on MSN with messages back and forth, flirtations, the whole thing, and then she met the guy and of course she was extremely disappointed, having built it all up.

In some senses it is a numbers game because it's about seeing whether this person you are applying to is a fit, so the sooner you know that the sooner you can move on to the next one. Why waste your time? It's about finding the right person, after all!

Trisha Stone, singles coach

TRISHA'S SNAPSHOT

I've been twice divorced and then in a relationship for three years that I knew wasn't right but I stayed in it. Then I did my coach training and then came across this programme with the Relationship Coaching Institute in the USA. I did the programme, applied it and then met my partner within two months.

I met him on the internet. I think you have to apply the same criteria – you have to be perceptive about what people are saying though you can do a lot of digging in their profile, all that sort of thing, but when you meet them you have to know what you want to find out about them. You mustn't get carried away with the internet dating thing because people get into fantasies in their heads.

Meeting my partner the way I did makes me realise how possible it is – not just to meet someone but the right person. You are never too old to learn. I was over 50 when we met so I hope that fact might give encouragement to others.

Carol's story

Age at first marriage: 19; age at first break-up: 34
Age at second marriage: 38; age at second break-up: 48

Any children?

None

What was the cause of the split?

In my first marriage, my husband had an affair with his sister's best friend. I was not interested in having a family, he was.

In the second marriage, he had an affair (although claimed, as men do, that there was no one else involved). His view was that the joy had gone out of the marriage. He expected it to be moonlight, romance and roses all the time, whereas I believe that relationships evolve. I gave up a high-powered job in the BBC to work locally in order to spend more time with him, but he could not handle the high local profile that this gave me. In short, he was jealous.

In public he behaved very badly and in both public and private he bullied me. I failed to see this until long after the relationship was dead. What I did not acknowledge was that as a perfectionist I am a workaholic and carry that perfectionism into any hobbies or interests. In many cases my work and life do not divide neatly into two halves, which clearly some men are unable to understand.

What efforts did you make individually or as a couple to save the marriage?

First time round, very little. After he literally threw me out, he used to come round to where I was staying and harass me, begging me to come back even though he had almost moved the about-to-be second wife into our marital home.

Second time round I tried hard to persuade him that we had a future. He was adamant that we did not – and with the benefit of hindsight it is easy to see why.

If you turned to professionals, in what ways did they help?

I used a conciliation service for sorting out details of the second divorce. I also suggested counselling but he would not entertain the idea.

In the division of the spoils, neither party felt we'd done as well as we should, which is usually how solicitors think they have got it about right.

How did you sort out the finances?

First time round it was long and drawn out with a very unsatisfactory outcome. I left with less than I brought to the marriage, no home and no career, so it was a case of starting again from scratch.

Second time round it was not particularly amicable. He would often be very tearful, a form of emotional blackmail I suppose, but conciliation certainly shortened the process and made it cheaper.

How were you affected, emotionally and physically, by the split?

In both cases I was emotionally devastated and I lost a lot of weight.

How did you cope when you were living alone?

I got a new job and made a new start the first time. Second time round I was able to continue doing what I was doing, move to a new house, move on with a new set of friends and leave bad memories behind.

Would you have done anything differently?

I probably would have fought much harder for a better settlement the first time round, but was so browbeaten and shocked that I was forced to back off and accept a very bad deal, feeling I couldn't face a fight. I think this was the wrong decision but I did not have the mental or emotional stamina for a fight at that time. I suspect that is a common feeling for a lot of people.

How long did it take to put your life back together, or at least to feel like facing the world?

It was three or four months until I felt like facing the world again, longer to put my life back on track. I felt great loathing and anger, but mostly very deep hurt, while trying to recognise that there is always fault on both sides. I had to start from scratch – new career, somewhere to live, learning to be impoverished again.

The second time was easier as I buried myself in my work (which I think can be dangerous) and stayed in the family home until it was sold. This took a year, so it was not until I moved that I felt I had really moved on.

I made so many sacrifices for him but now I actually feel sorry for him as he is clearly an inadequate man when it comes to relationships with very unreal expectations. He is married for the third time, living in France, but still contacts me, having heard that I am suffering from leukaemia. I have told him several times that he is no longer part of my life but he persists in emailing me. I usually delete his emails unread.

How has your life evolved since the break-up?

I have found new relationships, but as a very self-sufficient person the business of living on my own is not an issue. By having to work and being very single-minded about rebuilding a career I am probably better on my own. I don't live full-time with my current partner; we are both writers so better understand the demands and pressures each has. A small group of girlfriends have also been very supportive in the second case, although after the first marriage my forced move, and penury, led to setting up a whole new set of friends and support network.

Any advice for others?

- Always believe in yourself.

- Learn to respect yourself (assuming that you are the dumped one rather than the dumper).

- It is all right to be selfish and indulge yourself occasionally, particularly if it helps to boost morale.

- Don't rush into new relationships; that way often leads to disaster and more pain.

- There is no stigma in being single. Enjoy and value your independence, particularly if, like me, you don't have any children.

- Listen to and value your friends, even if sometimes they are saying things that you would rather not hear. It is never too late to make new friends, or a new life, however black things may seem at times. My experience is that new friends come from the most unexpected places.

- Don't blame yourself.

- Don't trust your partner when they say there is no one else involved – that's never the case!

- Try to accept your own faults and the fact that the reasons why the marriage failed may have something to do with you, somewhere along the line. I am a firm believer that most marriage breakdowns are cases of six of one and half-a-dozen of the other. This is often not outwardly the case but dig a little deeper and you have to see the flaws in yourself, and try to learn from those mistakes and not repeat them.

Making the most of yourself

When your emotions have taken a battering, feeling confident about the way you look and present yourself to the world is often a long way down your list of priorities. Just getting through each day takes all your effort in the early stages. But it's often then, when you look in the mirror, that you see yourself at your lowest and worst, causing that oh-so-fragile self-esteem to plummet yet further.

Action is called for. There is so much you can do for yourself – from top to toe – that can make a positive difference, and it needn't cost a lot in time or money. Taking care with your diet and general health is of paramount importance, and hopefully everything else will stem from that. Regular exercise, whether that's a brisk half-hour walk each day or something more structured like the gym or swimming sessions, will help you tone up and give you an appetite for a diet of mainly fresh food that includes plenty of fruit and vegetables. This will in turn enhance your skin, improve the workings of your internal organs and give you a glow that sends out the message: "I'm fine and I'm feeling good, thank you very much."

If time and money are not in short supply you may want to join the many others who turn to cosmetic enhancement as a way of boosting their self-confidence post-divorce.

Back in the singles market and eager for a mate, women are increasingly choosing to go under the knife in the hope of improving their chances of finding happiness.

The most popular procedures among divorcees are said to be breast enhancement and liposuction, closely followed by facial surgery, including eye bag removal.

There are also increasing numbers of women, fresh out of relationships, who turn to non-surgical procedures, including Botox and facial peels, to give them the self-assurance they need before they launch themselves into the dating game.

Callum's story

Age at marriage: 28
Age at break-up: 40

Any children?
Three, aged 12, 10 and eight

What was the cause of the split?
It became apparent that my wife had been insecure from her childhood and made progressively greater demands on me. She verged on the unstable, becoming something of a hypochondriac. I came to realise that staying together for the sake of the children could be corrosive for all of us.

What efforts did you make individually or as a couple to save the marriage?
We went to Relate sessions. In private discussions, it transpired that as a child she had been told by her mother that she was less capable than her siblings.

If you turned to professionals, in what ways did they help?

The counselling sessions had little effect, mainly because my wife could not accept that there was any action she could take.

How did you sort out the financial and residence issues?

As I felt the children were better together, I made the house over to my wife and supported the children. This was confirmed by my wife's solicitor through a court order. I had regular access to the children and took them on annual holidays.

How were you affected, emotionally and physically, by the split?

I was very concerned for my children but I was fortunate to have the support of a woman I subsequently met (whom I later married) and between us we put a lot of effort into our relationship with our children (she had two of her own). There was a time when we feared we had driven them away, but with continuing love they all now get on well with us.

How did you cope when you were living alone?

I was fortunate that I never really lived a 'single' life. My friendship with the woman who was to become my second wife ensured I always experienced loving support, from the early days onwards.

Would you have done anything differently?

I got married the first time believing that I could build a loving relationship from scratch. I was attracted to an idea, a dream. Having now experienced the real thing, I realise that then we had little chance and the bedrock of a marriage should be a lot of mutual respect and, ideally, love.

How long did it take to put your life back together, or at least to feel like facing the world?

Three to four years. I was fortunate that I met the woman who was to become my wife at a critical time. It involved a tremendous amount of heartache, which would have been very painful had we not had each other. But 20 years down the line we know it was the right thing for us.

How has your life evolved since the break-up?

The aggro we endured as we coped with the ending of our respective marriages and the building of our new relationship actually helped cement us together. I particularly enjoy the very positive friendships we have been able to build with our respective children.

Any advice for others?

- You need good friends

- Don't overlook the help the church could give you. We were fortunate that we had ministers at our church who were able to give us a lot of their time and support. Even if you do not belong to a church, most vicars/ministers can help. While they support the institution of marriage, they are realistic enough to understand human frailties.

- Try to be as unselfish as possible without being a martyr. That's what we say to people when they come to us and ask how we managed, perhaps contemplating a similar situation themselves and thinking we might have the answer. But there isn't one answer because every situation is different.

Tanya's story

Age at marriage: 25
Age at break-up: 48

Any children?

Three, aged 19, 18 and 13

What was the cause of the split?

My husband's infidelity. He had always been a flirt but in an innocent way, or so I thought. However, he had an affair with the local doctor's wife. I found out about it through an anonymous letter enclosing photos taken of her arriving at my house while I was away.

What efforts did you make individually or as a couple to save the marriage?

We regrouped. He stopped seeing the woman (I think) but the damage was done and all trust gone. I found it difficult to be civil to him. A year or so later he left me, not for her but for an old family friend whose husband had left her.

If you turned to professionals, in what ways did they help?

After the split I saw a therapist. It didn't help much, possibly because I felt I hadn't chosen the right one to go to.

My solicitor made it very clear to from the start that divorce was purely about sorting out the finances. Indeed this is what it proved to be. Now, I would favour mediation over solicitors, certainly at the beginning (and I am told it's less expensive).

How did you sort out the financial and residence issues?

None of the legalities took a very long time but it wasn't at all amicable – at least not until we realised how expensive a divorce was. Despite all the legal work that had been done, we settled the finances ourselves with one phone call. It certainly saved us money by settling out of court.

I got the house but not much money, so soon had to move to realise some capital. Luckily, I had a part-time job.

Custody was not an issue as the boys didn't want to see their father. They were very angry with him and refused to see his new partner. However, over a period of time this changed and things are fine now. They have a good relationship with him but I think they will always miss the 'united family'.

How were you affected, emotionally and physically, by the split?

Very badly. I was an emotional wreck, lost masses of weight and took to chain smoking. I felt very lonely, especially as it was when the two older children were leaving home.

How did you cope when you were living alone?

I had always paid the bills and run the house, so that was not a problem. Loneliness was the main issue and my social life came to a standstill. I longed for my previous life.

I continued as best as I could to work, play sport and go out. I am definitely someone who enjoys 'sharing' my life and you cannot put this onus on your children. I have been lucky enough to meet other men, but you have to make the effort.

Would you have done anything differently?

I don't regret my first marriage and love my three sons with a passion. I don't think that a bit of unfaithfulness is as bad I used to think and should not necessarily break up a marriage. Communication is very important and if we had communicated more about our feelings we might have avoided the break-up.

I wish I had tried harder to keep the family together as I truly rate family life. I think the children have had unnecessary pressure which I was fortunate enough not to suffer as I came from a stable home.

I certainly regret rushing into a second marriage. Better to keep it as a 'relationship' as it is simpler to get out of if it fails.

How long did it take to put your life back together, or at least to feel like facing the world?

Years, certainly not months. Time, I think, is a good healer. I stopped harbouring any feelings of anger or hate and realised I'd got over the break-up when I entered a new relationship.

It is fortunate that my ex-husband has had no more children as that could have created difficulties for me and my children.

How has your life evolved since the break-up?

My involvement in a new relationship led to marriage, which sadly did not last. I am single again now but am happy and confident. I do have a new man in my life but it is not 24/7 and marriage will be out of the question.

Any advice for others?

- Keep open the lines of communication with your ex for the sake of the children.

- Never be critical of your ex to the children.

- Don't do anything rash or in a hurry. Take time to make considered moves and decisions.

- Take each day as it comes and with time it really does get better.

- Make an effort to meet someone else – but don't rush into remarriage.

EXTRA HELP

There are more internet dating sites than you could shake a hopeful stick at: a search via Google will yield many hundreds, but you may wish to narrow your search to those which attract people with interests that match or at least complement yours, perhaps who read the same newspaper [try Guardian Soulmates] or who are strict vegans or keen bikers. Somewhere, out there in the ether, your intended could be waiting for you to click.

CHAPTER 7

Your personal recovery kit

There are as many ways of getting over a separation or divorce as there are people who go through it. A 'one size fits all' fix-and-repair kit is patently not an option, but a 'pick and mix' method certainly is.

You have read what's on offer in this book, so now you can choose what you think best suits you and your circumstances, discard the bits that don't appeal, and put together your own first-aid kit for recovery. This might include three or four websites to explore, a couple of telephone helplines to call, a few aphorisms to memorise, some case studies that inspire you, and half-a-dozen phrases to guide you from the experts whose professional advice is featured in each chapter.

Perhaps most importantly of all, don't forget to make room in your recovery kit for these:

20 top tips to aid recovery

1 Take responsibility for yourself.

2 Be self-reliant. It's more peaceful.

3 Know that the black tunnel is something you will emerge from.

4 Try to move on as quickly as you can, say thank you for what was good and don't bear grudges.

5 Remember you are a person with a life and this is not a rehearsal.

6 Cherish your friends. They may be lonely too. Assure them that they can retain friendships with both you and your ex-partner.

7 Do not condemn the other parent in the presence of the children.

8 When it's all really, really ghastly at the beginning, learn to tackle only that day's problems. Next week's or next month's issues can wait.

9 Try not to feel bitter because it harms you more than anyone else.

10 Prioritise your own health and wellbeing.

11 Seek advice. There are plenty of organisations that can help.

12 Look forward without regret.

13 Try to avoid the things that can make you feel very fed up and sorry for yourself, like doing the supermarket shop at 2am.

14 Don't think you are alone.

15 Be selfish, in the best sense of the word.

16 Remember: there is no stigma in being single.

17 Don't do anything rash or in a hurry. Take time to make considered moves and decisions.

18 Just stick in there and believe in your ability to withstand whatever is thrown at you.

19 Keep optimistic – life is full of surprises.

20 Always remember: things will get better.

(With thanks to all the case study volunteers for these.)

And finally ... one more for luck

21 Smile – it's your smile and no one can take *that* away from you.

Contact us

You're welcome to contact White Ladder Press if you have any questions or comments for either us or the authors. Please use whichever of the following routes suits you.

Phone 01803 813343

Email enquiries@whiteladderpress.com

Fax 01803 813928

Address White Ladder Press, Great Ambrook, Near Ipplepen, Devon TQ12 5UL

Website www.whiteladderpress.com

What can our website do for you?

If you want more information about any of our books, you'll find it at **www.whiteladderpress.com**. In particular you'll find extracts from each of our books, and reviews of those that are already published. We also run special offers on future titles if you order online before publication. And you can request a copy of our free catalogue.

Many of our books have links pages, useful addresses and so on relevant to the subject of the book. You'll also find out a bit more about us and, if you're a writer yourself, you'll find our submission guidelines for authors. So please check us out and let us know if you have any comments, questions or suggestions.